This Way Home

Selected *and* New Work

ESSENTIAL POETS SERIES 289

Canada

ONTARIO ARTS COUNCIL
CONSEIL DES ARTS DE L'ONTARIO
an Ontario government agency
un organisme du gouvernement de l'Ontario

Canada Council for the Arts
Conseil des arts du Canada

Guernica Editions Inc. acknowledges the support of
the Canada Council for the Arts and the Ontario Arts Council.
The Ontario Arts Council is an agency of the Government of Ontario.
We acknowledge the financial support of the Government of Canada

Gianna Patriarca

This Way Home

Selected *and* New Work

GUERNICA
EDITIONS

TORONTO • CHICAGO
BUFFALO • LANCASTER (U.K.)
2021

Michael Mirolla, editor
Cover and interior design: Rafael Chimicatti
Cover photo: Andrew Milne-Allan
Author photo: Paul Salvatori
Guernica Editions Inc.
287 Templemead Dr., Hamilton, Ontario, Canada L8W 2W4
2250 Military Road, Tonawanda, N.Y. 14150-6000 U.S.A.
www.guernicaeditions.com

Distributors:
Independent Publishers Group (IPG)
600 North Pulaski Road, Chicago IL 60624
University of Toronto Press Distribution (UTP)
5201 Dufferin Street, Toronto (ON), Canada M3H 5T8
Gazelle Book Services, White Cross Mills
High Town, Lancaster LA1 4XS U.K.

First edition.
Printed in Canada.

Legal Deposit – Third Quarter
Library of Congress Catalog Card Number: 2021932964
Library and Archives Canada Cataloguing in Publication
Title: This way home : selected and new work / Gianna Patriarca.
Other titles: Poems. Selections
Names: Patriarca, Gianna, author.
Series: Essential poets ; 289.
Description: First edition. | Series statement: Essential poets series ; 289
Identifiers: Canadiana 2021014064X | ISBN 9781771836708 (softcover)
Classification: LCC PS8581.A6665 A6 2021 | DDC C811/.6—dc23

in memory of
my grandparents

Angela Maria Martini and Arduino Ignagni
Giacinta Maiuri and Giacomo Patriarca

they loved me enough to lie

i am not really there.
that is what tires me. invisibility.
it is exhausting.

—Pier Giorgio Di Cicco
(the honeymoon wilderness)

Whatever it was happened:
the battle, the sunny day, the moonlit
slipping into lust, the farewell kiss.

—Margaret Atwood
(Dearly)

Preface

Gianna Patriarca: Identity in Language

Gianna Patriarca is an award-winning writer and author of nine books of poetry and prose; she has, as well, authored essays and other work directed toward children. Because of such an enduring career of three decades to date, the quality of her work and such bountiful production have positioned her as one of Canada's more recognized and impactful voices. Yet, she has, like many hyphenated writers, borne the burden of that diacritical mark. This is not a rare phenomenon and, further still, it is not only Canadian. I would contend here that we are dealing with a grave circumstance that is both North American — Canada and the United States — and anglophone in origin.

The decades-long struggle of the Italian/Canadian writer — poet especially — is not dissimilar to what we have witnessed in the United States.[1] If the "Italian" writer is not overtly stereotypical, her/his collection of poetry or fiction may not pass muster with those readers who are, for all practical purposes, the Cerberuses at the gate who prevent the manuscript from moving forward. In an interview about this very experience, Gianna rightfully acknowledged the challenge. When asked if "literature with Italian Canadian themes deserves a place in the Canadian literary canon," she responded:

> I have often stated that we (Italian/Canadian writers) are easily dismissed here in Canada. (I have had personal experiences where this was clearly apparent). We have been grouped in a category of writers as "unoriginal" and this really angers me. It seems

1 My use of the slash (/) in place of the hyphen (-) has its origins in my essays, *To Hyphenate or not to Hyphenate: the Italian/American Writer: Or, An* Other *American?* (Montreal: Guernica Editions, 1991).

> because we have, as an immigrant group, been successful and have established ourselves in prominent businesses, etc., our stories don't seem relative or tragic enough to stand up as literature, as if our struggle has been erased as if it was irrelevant. Someone once said to me: "Italian Canadian writers are just whiners, what have you got to complain about?" That sort of ignorance pretty much outlines it all.[2]

At the risk of seeming like one of those a "whiners," I strongly contend that there is much truth to her two thoughts, that Italian/Canadians are: (1) "grouped in a category of writers as 'unoriginal'" and (2) "as an immigrant group [...] have established [them]selves in prominent businesses, etc." The unspoken, I would contend, is that the very Italian/North American reading public — both in Canada and in the United States — is part of the issue. The desire to acculturate, if not assimilate, bumps up against the hyphen and all that it entails, and, as a result, the ethnic is often sidelined. One remedy, I would suggest, is the greater propagation of such literature, which can only educate those who are not in the know.

This Way Home is an antidote to such cultural ignorance and biases; it speaks to the universal on the one hand, yet, it also speaks not only to the particularity of gender but to gender within an Italian hyphenated semiosphere. Thus, the reader in the end comes to know about the universalities of gender, for instance, through the lens of a hyphenated perspective of the Italian migratory act and other issues pertinent to said phenomena.

I began my comments with a reference to the oft dominant cultural dismissal of the "hyphenate writer" because of a pesky diacritical mark. But, as I suspect we all would agree, literature is a thematically based neutral platform to which the writer brings a series of expressions — rhetorical strategies, if you will — of those thoughts, concepts, and experiences s/he wishes to articulate. This

2 Domenico Capolongo, "Un momento with Gianna Patriarca." http://italocanadese.com/2012/10/15/un-momento-with-gianna-patriarca. Accessed November 23, 2020.

is what Gianna Patriarca does in her writing; her work is universal in theme with an Italian flair, the ideal succession of characteristics to anyone's successful written forms, be they in verse or in prose, or some combination thereof. It is the universal that attracts and holds the attention of the general reader, while the particular — in this case the Italian — helps maintain said attention and, to boot, educates the reader about said particularities.

***

This Way Home opens with poems from her first collection, *Italian Women and Other Tragedies*, and closes with the inclusion of some of her most recent poems composed after her latest publication, *To The Men Who Write Good-bye Letters* (2020). They are lyrical compositions of the same intensity as we have witnessed in her previous poetry. Free verse, sparing use of capital letters, keen inclusion of blank spaces between words of the same verse, and seemingly simple words that communicate the most profound of thoughts.

All this adds to the unique voice that is Gianna Patriarca. As she did in her debut collection, *Italian Women and Other Tragedies*, Gianna continued to explore in subsequent books those basic themes that constitute her identity as an Italian/Canadian woman. Not just her first book, but all of Gianna's poetry is an existential voyage of an immigrant woman's physical and emotional journey[s]. This is what we find in *This Way Home*; on the one hand, a testimonial to the story of a woman born in a small town in the province of Frosinone, east of Rome and, on the other, the chronicling of the gender aspect of our narrator's migratory Italian/Canadian existence and her subsequent life experiences in Canada.

As shall become apparent, the foundation of Patriarca's poetry is twofold in nature. It is, on the one hand, a physical/sentimental trajectory of women whose existence, precisely because they are women, is situated in a de-privileged and disenfranchised socio-familial position vis-à-vis their male counterparts. On the other hand, as I had suggested elsewhere, Patriarca's trajectory is also epistemological: as a woman in a man's world, she has stepped over the Cartesian threshold of *Cogito ergo sum.*[3] She now "thinks"; she has constructed an "Andersdenken, un altro pensiero, il pensiero dell'altro," as Franco Rella tells us is necessary.[4] In this Cartesian dependence on Reason and because of her discovery of thought, the "other thought" especially, Patriarca has set up her own cognitive process based on her gender specificity. Her semiotic interaction with the world around her, then, can only be one of strife and struggle regardless of any desire for the opposite, precisely because she is "other" of the "pensiero dell'altro" that we saw above. It is thus this "other" thought that constitutes Patriarca's epistemological tragedy.[5]

As we read from collection to collection about her life and poetry, we come to understand how Gianna has negotiated her position as both human being and writer in her seemingly forever-newly-founded land of Canada. Included in this collection from *My Etruscan Face* (2007) is the poem "i am *ciociara*" in both English and in the Ciociaria dialect. In reading this poem, which is approximately half-way through Gianna's multi-decade-long lyrical trajectory, we find our narrating voice still dealing with identity as an emigrant ("I went away / [...] / you stayed home") compared to those who stayed. The results of the migratory act are multiple and challenging, to say the least. The migrant is "without a history / or an education" because she is forced to leave for "somewhere far." Indeed, her communication with those who stay ("i read the words you write and / feel abandoned one more time") only add to the feeling of estrangement, the difference between the emigrant and

3 See my *A Semiotic of Ethnicity: In (Re)cognition of the Italian/American Writer* (Albany, NY: SUNY Press) chap. 6.

4 Franco Rella, *Miti e figure del moderno* (Milan: Feltrinelli, 1993, 2nd edition), p. 26; italics textual. Rella goes on to quote Benjamin, that this "pensiero dell'altro," according to the German philosopher, is "il pensiero di ciò che non è stato mai scritto" (p. 26).

5 Here I am using Rella' s concept of tragedy in order to localize and particularize a certain relationship between it and Patriarca's cognitive poetic world. Rella, in fact, states: "La tragedia non è la narrazione di eventi luttuosi: è un pensiero. E' il pensiero che fluidifica i confini conosciuti, tra la polis e ciò che è estemo alla polis, tra maschile e femminile, tra umano e divino. E' il pensiero che scopre che il rapporto dell'uomo [sic] con il mondo e con il divino si realizza dentro un conflitto" (p. 15).

the one who stayed behind ("you have a history").[6] The emigrant is cut off from the "little town" where she "wanted to stay home too." But she could not ("i didn't have a house / [...] / my father was ... / somewhere far"). Distance and hence separation underscore the sense of not having a history ("you have a history") and being "condemned," as she writes, to "invent" her own history in this anglophone semiosphere that is not hers, and hence she is "broken" like the language in which she now communicates ("broken dialect / i write").

This sense of alienation recalls a United States writer, among many, who has bemoaned the phenomenon of being "plucked" from his own village, "deracinated," as Joseph Tusiani wrote in his canonical Italian/American "Song of the Bicentennial."[7] Our *ciociara* in this poem is indeed the result of the outer imposed migratory act that leaves the emigrant without a "history" forced continually to write her own: "i keep inventing mine." Let us not lose the significance of the insistent on the continuation of the act; we read "i *keep* inventing" and not an articulation of a past act of having had to invent one's history. The migratory act is a perennial experience, as we read the last verse of the poem: "how condemned i *am*" (emphasis mine).

Early on, we find an analogous empathetic testament to the father's broken spirit, afflicted by thirty years of being elsewhere, as her use and juxtaposition of certain words punctuate the immigrant's dilemma. Indeed, the adjective for the present, foreign, is now synonymous with old and conjures up notions of futility and despair; whereas the adjective for the past, young, is synonymous with *new* and conversely conjures up the notion of possibility and hope. But, in the end, all hope is lost ("rotted"), as the immigrant does not, perhaps cannot, return to his native land:

---

6 With regard to identity in the collection *My Etruscan Face*, see Deborah Saidero, "The Transcultural Rewriting of the Italian Ethnoscape," *Oltreoceano* 7 (2013): 57-66.

7 For more on this poem, see my "Joseph Tusiani's *Gente Mia*: Coincidences of E(im)migration" in Anthony Julian Tamburri, *Re-reading Italian Americana: Specificities and Generalities on Literature and Criticism* (Madison, NJ: Fairleigh Dickinson University Press, 2014).

but for thirty years now
he's slept in a foreign bed
that has curved his spine

the corn husks of his young bed
have rotted in a cradle
if he could return
to smell the earth
his father left him
he would understand

All this because the "return," as we are told ("Returning"), is "the other dream," for which "other" is another form of impossibility for these old immigrants who no longer "discuss the distance anymore" since for them it is no longer a reality; "it has lost its nationality." The "distance" that these immigrants no longer discuss represents as well the very difference between them and the new world in which they live. They do not "discuss the difference" precisely because they have not developed that "altro pensiero," as has instead our female narrator.

Identity returns at the end of *This Way Home* in the section dedicated to her latest collection *To the Men Who Write Goodbye Letters*. A collection that comes after more than two decades of writing poetry, we find a plethora of thematics that, overall, deal with endings. One of these poems that stands out in relation to what we have said above is the immigrant's sense of identity. Indeed, the very title of the poem declares the theme, "Identity." It is the identity of the female migrant of two different generations:

Identity

my mother   did not fall
into sentiment   or romance
                          easily
had no doubts
knew   who she was
[…]

unlike me   i question everything
find   few answers
i cry in the daylight
        my mother cried in the dark

The migrant mother who came as an adult could not "fall / into sentiment   or romance" because according to tradition, she was who she was, the above-mentioned disenfranchised vis-à-vis their male counterparts, something we saw in Gianna's first collection. The subjection of the female at that time was sometimes accompanied by violence, as we saw then in the poem "Italian Women":

these are the women
who were born to give birth

they breathe only
leftover air
and speak only
when deeper voices
have fallen asleep

i have seen them bleed
in the dark

Like the narrator's mother who "cried in the dark," the women of Gianna's first collection bled "in the dark." The new generation, we see in the later poem, "question[s] everything," just as the younger woman of *Italian Women and Other Tragedies* went against cultural norms and paid dearly, as we saw in the poem "Daughters":

a young Italian woman's
claim to prostitution
is any activity past
the midnight hour

his eyes were coral
as he rammed the fist
inside my mouth
reminding me

and my mother screamed

[...]

if only i could be more
like my married sister
or the virgin daughters
of the virgin neighbours

and how did the Devil
come to live inside our house?

and my mother prays

***

Tied to any notion of identity is language, be that Italian, dialect, or some form of the language of the host country, in our case English. One example early on of language and identity vis-à-vis immigrant worker's plight she presents in "*Dolce-Amaro*" (*Italian Women and Other Tragedies*), a tribute to her father's experience of close to thirty years "under the white weight / of endless Januarys":

this country has taken everything
his health, his language
the respect of his modem children
the love of his angry wife.

By their positionality of being enumerated as first and second, "health" and "language" are given primacy of value, two essentially physical characteristics that supersede emotional elements such as "respect" and "love" between the father and his children and wife. In her second collection, *Daughters for Sale*, language is primary once more in "The Last Confession," as the old female narrator in the nursing home shares with her reader: "will they understand / i do not have my language anymore."

In her third collection, *Ciao, Baby*, language takes on two functions: one of identity, the other for communication, in the poem "Notes on Aging":

> my aunt will never know
> i write *poems* for her
> her life without *metaphors*
> lived with the *rhythm* of a *broken language*
> thirty years spent in airless factories
> my dying aunt will not *read* my poems
> but i know her life helped me
> *write* them
>
> (my emphasis)

The "broken language" is an obvious allusion to the immigrant aunt's English in this new world. But it is, in this instance, curiously attached to writing, indeed insofar as to the allusion of writing poetry: "rhythm of a broken language." And this seemingly aesthetic allusion has an added object to the original one of the immigrant's language. Now, bracketed literally between verses that contain the word "poems," as we see above, "language" now references communication at this juncture, a communication, we need add, about the aesthetic act of writing and — as well, reading — verse. Our narrator "write[s] poems" for her aunt, who will never "read [such] poems." But it is "her life without metaphors" that is the muse of our narrator's poetry — "her life helped me / write them." As such, then, this immigrant's "broken language" is no longer broken; as the muse of her niece's poetry, the aunt's own language "without metaphors" is now metaphorically transposed from a level of basic communication to one of an aesthetic act, through which, a reader might supersede — that is, interpret — the seemingly random propinquity at first blush of these words in this stanza.

This instance of staggered positioning of significant words sets up a linearity that we might not often recognize after our first reading. In case of the eight verses cited above, we may formulate the following affirmation of the poet's aesthetics: The poet offers *poems* written in order to infuse *metaphor* and *rhythm* in a *broken language* that, once *read*, we may then understand why the *poems* were *written*. An act of interpretive prestidigitation, one might ask? Not really! Language is, for Gianna, the core vehicle through which we articulate our thoughts and feelings. "[L]anguage is always an issue," we read in "Second Language" (*Ciao, Baby*). Language is both vehicle for and, as a conglomeration of signs, depository of our thoughts and feelings. This is what her "arms can [and do] carry" ("What My Arms Can Carry" [*What My Arms Can Carry*]). For language, we come to understand at this stage in Gianna's lyrical journey, is all of who we are, as the narrator states:

> i am a name and a landscape
> a language and a dialect
> i am memory and history
> the present and the future

Language as depository of who we are is underscored even at the later stage of Patriarca's career. In "Language" (*To The Men Who Write Goodbye Letters*), we come to understand the specificities of different languages, and that when they disappear so do our identities:

> this new world has no need for
> old languages
> but while i am here
> i will hold it safe
> in the limbo of my gut

And as she locks the door to her dead mother's house, our narrator tells us:

> i am left to empty my mother's
> house of all the years
> language   history

The verse/couplet, "language history," encapsulates the essential relationship between language and identity. Who we are is signaled through and/or marked by our language: our language articulates our history, our history is articulated through our language. We thus can modify Descartes's proverbial "Cogito ergo sum" into "Loquor ergo sum," for which language (*loquor*) and identity (*sum*) are inseparable, as she wrote this very past year in the poem "Modern Wedding in a City Loft":

> no one really noticed grandmother
> was there
> [...]
> no one spoke her language

The absence of one ("no one spoke her language") leads to the absence of the other ("no one really noticed grandmother").

Gianna's creativity transcends the story she wants to tell. Along with what she wants to say, her creative originality is equally rooted in how she says what she says. Gianna's language is, on the surface, straightforward, which, along with its recall of realistic narrative prose, has an artistic function. It adds a certain realistic tone to Patriarca's frequent narrative technique of non-linearity. Within a framework of seemingly direct language combined with her use of gut-wrenching imagery, Patriarca succeeds in portraying problematic situations of human interactions, specifically, gender issues and family relationships. Whereas narration, in both prose and poetry, tends to be more descriptive than expressive, Gianna's narration maintains its descriptive component while adding an explicitly expressive one. Namely, form and content become intricately engaged so that the one is always de-pendent on the existence of the other; the work of art cannot stand alone, as *ars gratia artis* is not consonant with Gianna's poetics. Something of which she is well aware is the intricate relationship of art and life:

> i think of poems i might write
> but there is no image
> for this moment

for who she is
my only daughter
my prayer
the greatest poem of my life.

The result is an intensely emotional, quasi-visual work of art — in this case, poetry — that engages the reader in its communicative act: the reader, that is, becomes a co-participant in the poems point of view and signifying act and therefore experiences the narrator's emotional *iter*.

Anthony Julian Tamburri
Dean, John D. Calandra Italian American Institute
Distinguished Professor of European Languages and Literatures

Anthony Julian Tamburri is Dean of the John D. Calandra Italian American Institute (Queens College, CUNY) and Distinguished Professor of European Languages and Literatures. He is co-founder of Bordighera Press, past president of the Italian American Studies Association and of the American Association of Teachers of Italian. His latest books include: *Scrittori Italiano[-]Americani: trattino sì trattino no* (2018), *Un biculturalismo negato: La scrittura "italiana" negli Stati Uniti* (2018); and *Signing Italian/American Cinema: A More Focused Look* (2021). He is executive producer and host of the Calandra Institute's TV program, *Italics*, produced in collaboration with CUNY TV. He also writes a column for *La Voce di New York*, entitled "The Italian Diaspora."

Contents

from: Italian Women and Other Tragedies

from: Daughters for Sale

from: Ciao Baby

from: What My Arms Can Carry

from: The Invisible Woman

from: My Etruscan Face

from: Too Much Love

from: Donne Italiane ed Altre Tragedie (Italian translation)

from: To The Men Who Write Goodbye Letters

New poems/2020

from:

Italian Women and Other Tragedies

Italian Women

these are the women
who were born to give birth

they breathe only
leftover air
and speak only
when deeper voices
have fallen asleep

i have seen them bleed
in the dark
hiding the stains inside them
like sins
apologizing

i have seen them wrap their souls
around their children
and serve their hearts
in a meal they never
share

My Birth

my father is a great martyr
he has forgiven me everything
even my female birth

January was a bitch of a month
when i raised my head, for the
first time
from my mother's stained and
aching womb

a dozen relatives waited in the kitchen
to see the prize in the Easter egg

how i disappointed them
my father's first child
was not male

i swear i can still hear the
only welcoming sounds
were from my mother
and she has always been blamed
for the mistake

for weeks
my father was drunk on red wine
mourning the loss of his immortality

Daughters

my father called me whore
and my mother cried

a young Italian woman's
claim to prostitution
is any activity past
the midnight hour

his eyes were coral
as he rammed his fist
inside my mouth
reminding me

and my mother screamed

the walls are knocking
how will they face the
neighbours in the morning

if only i could be more
like my married sister
or the virgin daughters
of the virgin neighbours

and how did the Devil
come to live inside our house?
and my mother prays

May/Maggio

the trees
have finally decided
to laugh

the way my mother laughed
before the changes
the new country

before she woke up to
the dark stranger
in her bed

before she recognized
my sister no longer cared
for ribbons

this month the
flowers appear most
beautiful

this month i can put
aside anything
i am drunk with trees

Maggio/May

gli alberi
hanno finalmente
deciso di ridere

come mia mamma rideva
prima del cambio
della nuova terra

prima di svegliarsi
accanto
allo scuro estraneo

prima di riconoscere
che mia sorella non
voleva più fiocchi

questo mese
i fiori appaiano
belli

questo mese
scanzerò tutto
sono ubriaca
di alberi

Contrasti

i am not the fine
white English flesh
that holds those eyes
the ones who borrowed
the clearest blue from
a Pacific island sky

i have not the small
gentle hands
you mistook for wild flowers
and photographed endlessly
in gardens   orchards
sleepy city lofts

i am not the one whose hair
ignites sun-fire in afternoons

i come to you from peasant stock
from gardens of large rocks
where thirsty flowers
lie un-photographed

For Roberto Pisapia

(resident of Villa Colombo)

you sit
flesh like stone
one leg less
a neighbour of death
your eyes draped by cataracts
they see me
but don't recognize the face
you smiled at for years
across a small table in the
neighbourhood café

Roberto, how quickly
time gives a final embrace

last July we laughed
talked of your days of song
with Caruso
the climbing lights on the head of Vesuvius
the streets of Naples flirting in the night

it is a long way from Naples
to Villa Colombo
here, they have built you a fountain
they place your wheelchair by its
ceramic border
i know your ears are fighting
its fraudulent sound

Roberto we will not speak again
until our eyes are the stars
over the Bay of Naples

Perhaps

perhaps my father would love
the colours of the olive trees
in summer

perhaps he would stop by the
slouching lazy leaves of a fig tree
close his eyes and remember
the dark haired children
climbing towards the sun

perhaps if he walked that road
of white pebbles
and reached the farmhouse
in the distance
he would touch the heads
of the new born chicks
and recall the wonder

but for thirty years now
he's slept in a foreign bed
that has curved his spine

the corn husks of his young bed
have rotted in a cradle

perhaps if he could return
to smell the earth
his father left him
he would understand

Returning

we don't discuss the distance anymore
returning is now
the other dream
not American at all
not Canadian or Italian
it has lost its nationality

in the sixties we came in swarms
like summer bees
smelling of something strange
wearing the last moist kiss
of our own sky
we came with heavy trunks
empty pockets
and a dream.
i was one of them
tucked away below the sea line
on the bottom floor of a ship
that swelled and ached
for thirteen days
our bellies emptied into the Atlantic
until the ship finally vomited
on the shores of Halifax
there, where the arms and legs
of my doll fell apart into the sea
finding their way back over the waves
my mother's young heart
wrapped around me
my sister crying
for *pane e mortadella*
we held on
two more nights

on a stiff cold train headed for
Toronto
where the open arms of a half-forgotten man
waited

Reasons

it really doesn't matter now
the reasons we left the fields
in all those towns cradled in
the gentle arms of green hills

the reasons we left the stone houses
we laughed in during the cold winters
where God was a fireplace

the reasons we left the hot summers
when finding water was a miracle
and we thanked the saints
and we thanks the priests
and we lit the candles

and when the bells sounded on Sunday mornings
we walked miles to thank the mass

it really doesn't matter now
if no one brings flowers to grandpa's grave
he never cared much for flowers anyway
and it won't matter if after you're gone
i won't remember your pain

you have always said that   i'm insensitive

i am part of this city now
the one that gives less than a damn
about our   reasons

The Garden

New Zealand gardens
are perfect
like the people
perfectly blonde
perfectly tall
perfectly gentle

in these gardens
my husband took shape
beneath this Pacific sun
that does not kill
the way the Italian sun
killed my ancestors
slowly

here the ground is alive
with roses and gum trees
that echo with magpies
but i remember rocks
large ones
my grandfather moved them
continually
but they always grew again

i lie here
among the wild agapanthus
beneath the red Pohutakawa
how did i come so far
from Lazio
to the bottom of the world
with a tall, light man
who smells of the sea

i am the dark rose
transplanted in this island
of the long white cloud

Sunday and You

take me there, my love
by the brook
beneath the white clouds
knitted in the summer sky

there, by the dry arms
of our tree
where i felt my limbs multiply
and root themselves in you

there, where the jealous sun
watched our eyes fly out
and become poems

and the gentle leaves
embarrassed by our kisses
made a game of our lives

i want to lie by the hem
of the brook with you
eating the sounds our
hearts make

one more time

For Grandma, in bed, waiting

your eyes are the wrong colour
there is no darkness in them
to write about
and pain is always dark
your smile comes too easily
pain never smiles
your face contradicts everything
yet, i know your heart is bruised
how can ninety-one years not have bruised
your tiny, fading body
that gave eight children to the world
and scattered thirty grandchildren
like wild flowers in foreign cities.
you have come to end your journey
uncomplaining
in this suburban bungalow
in a room with one window.
you don't always recognize me
but here is something between us
there is the touch of my fingers on
your perfect hand
i come to sit by your bed
not in duty
but in the need of the stories
that flow from you
i am in awe, i listen
you take me to your century
i will miss this journey
when you are gone.

The Poet

for Pier Giorgio

when i was twenty-six
i fell in love with a poet
he was tall and eloquent
and moved like a cloud
on a summer's day
his hands over the keyboard
were magic
and the poems appeared like
miracles
thousands of poems i understood
about the tragedy that was our
immigrant youth
the displacement of our hearts
the tears of our mothers
of young dead brothers
who lived in photographs
placed lovingly on altars
and on living room walls.
the poet made sense of our lives
gave us a place to fit and when
he moved away from the typewriter
satisfied
he'd light the cigarette
and speak to me of the country
that i was
the taste of things Italian
the songs of his grandfather
the ghosts of his past.
i took everything in

like a blessing
secure in my position.
when i was twenty-seven
the poet   left
to find other countries
to write about.

The Gift

you will not remember me
after this
i will be another
lifetime away

you will have slept
with one hundred
other women
and will have loved
each one
forever
as you loved me

do not lift your pillow
on nights you lie alone
you will find the light
from my eyes
will keep you   awake

Dolce-Amaro

he has learned to bend
the way branches do
under the white weight
of endless Januarys.
this country has taken everything
his health, his language
the respect of his modern children
the love of his angry wife.
in some forgotten lifetime
he was a young, dark-haired man
in a ship packed with young
dark-haired men
floating uncomfortably toward
a dream they didn't want to bury
with the still young bones
of mothers and fathers
among the ruins of a post-war Italy.
for most
the dream did not come easily
the golden paved North America
wasn't paved at all

only years of feeling strange
cold and hot months over multiplying bricks
hands turned leathery and large
needs stored away in cave cellars
deep, with the colour of aging wine.
in the evenings
there was the smell of group sweat
cheap meals seasoned with resentment
by the wives of aspiring landlords.
for my father

the dream ended early
when his knees were crushed
by the weight of steel
along some railroad line.
he was thirty-one
there was no insurance then
and little interest for the benefits
of an immigrant man.
he bends easily at fifty-seven
walks with a cane
rarely opens his lifeless eyes

the government sends him
fifty-one dollars a month
in recognition.

November 16, 1983

my father is dead
at sixty-one
his heart stopped
his truck stopped
death
at the traffic lights
of Lansdowne and St. Clair

four p.m.
alone
he didn't bother anyone
waited for the red light
so he would not disturb the
traffic
he was much more considerate
in death
than he had been in life

my father is dead
and i have nowhere
to put this anger

i was sure he would live
forever
to continue his battle
with me and my
poems

College Street, Toronto

i have come back to this street
to begin a new chapter of my inheritance
my Canadian odyssey.
for my father it began in 1956
in the basement of a Euclid Street
rooming house
with five other men
homeless, immigrant dreamers
bordanti
young, dark
handsome and strong
bricklayers
carpenters
gamblers.
they cooked their pasta
by the light of a forty watt bulb
drank bad red wine
as they argued the politics of
the country they left behind
avoiding always the new politics.
late in the evening they
spent their loose change
in the *Gatto Nero*, the *Bar Italia*
pool, espresso
cards and cigarettes
while in all the towns
from Friuli to Sicily
postponed families waited
for the letters, the dollars
the invitation.
then the exodus
of wives and children

trunks and wine glasses
hand stitched linens in hope chests
floating across the Atlantic
slowly
to Halifax
to Union Station
to College Street.
1960
my sister and i
cold and frightened
pushed toward a crowded gate
into the arms
of a strange man
who smelled of tobacco.
Crawford Street
three small rooms
in a three storey house
dark and airless
smelling of boiled fish
Rose and Louis Yutzman
lived downstairs
Louis died in the middle
of a frozen January night
Rose's screams were nails
driven hard into my eardrums.
my fearless mother
touched his silent face
held his limp, large hand
as she closed his eyes
while my father and i
barefoot and trembling
hid petrified behind the door.
we learned the language quickly
to everyone's surprise
my mother embraced her new life

in long factory lines
while my father continued his pleasures
in pool halls thick with voices
of other men in exile.
1981
the Italians are almost all gone
to new neighbourhoods
modern towns.
my father is gone
Bar Italia has a new clientele
women come here now
i come here
i drink espresso and smoke cigarettes

from the large window
that swims in sunlight
i think i see my father
leaning on the parking meter
passionately arguing
the soccer scores.
how strange this city
sometimes
it seems so much smaller
than all those towns
we came from.

Nina, la Matta

the neighbours think she's crazy
running out in the middle of the night
in her underwear
to hide in the garage
a wounded animal
hungry
for warmth and safety

they think her screams
are of a woman gone   mad
with superstition

she pours bags of salt
on the green grass around her house
to keep away the evil eye
there are crosses and beads
everywhere
knives in plastic bags
buried beneath her veranda

the neighbours know nothing
of the jagged glass
he tried to shove into her vagina
as their six year old son   watched
they know nothing of her beaten body
hurled down cellar stairs
like discarded work shoes

she walks to church each day
talking to the air
plastic flowers for the Madonna
she touches the blue marble gown

and then her lips
on her knees she walks the length
of the church for hours
everyone thinks she's   mad

Mary

Mary jumped
from stone to stone
small islands shining
in the August sun

she lost her balance
the water kissed her knees

i watched her
and loved her
the closest thing
to an angel
our fingers touching
we walked home

*

well little sister
it is the second year
of your new state
the woman
the wife
two years since you
dropped your laughter
in the music box
on the dresser
and walked out   smiling
in your white dress
with the thousand pearls
you left a shadow in our bedroom
that never sleeps

tonight i will stay
in another room

*

our bodies were foreign countries
never to be looked at
never to be touched
never to be understood

preserved in plastic
like Teresa's couch and chair
like her *giardiniera*
petrified in vinegar
to last forever
for some great   sacred
feast

Mary's breasts drip with
acid milk
she cannot feed her child
it will not nourish
it will not fill

her eyes are deep dark
question marks
she cannot control the hormones
going wild inside her veins
her tortured cry

my arms around her are a prayer
to flush out this devil
we do not understand
our hands bonded like children
i am here   please heal

*

she believes she's going crazy
but she doesn't know why
exploring the reasons
with each bead at her
fingertips
her life is perfect
she believes in God
and her husband

she adores the child
her home is comfortable
except she hates the kitchen

sitting by the light of the porch
staring into the dim suburban stars
the tears find their way into her lap
like large clear stones
perhaps tomorrow she will   smile
the pills will work
tomorrow

*

suburban grass is perfect
in a year my new nephew
will plant his knees everywhere
he will be green
like the neighbourhood

suburban flowers are neat
and quiet   they remind me
of my grandmother's hands
at the end

Mary sits
in the tall brittle shade
of her dried flowers
in her white living room
Van Gogh colours in her
eyes.

*

i visit often
to hold my new nephew
and to reminisce
of the days when we were
nieces
and all the living rooms
were open spaces.

Grace Street Summer

the moon is almost round tonight
a plane just flew over it
like a cartoon
lifting over Tony's garage
ripe as a honeydew melon
my thumb stretched out
we play hide-and-seek.
the schoolyard is loud
with boys and basketballs
in the distance Benny's radio
tuned to CHIN and Calabrian songs
his wife's voice in harmony
her doughy, round body
by the kitchen window
floating from sink to cupboard
dishes and cutlery being put to bed.
my daughter and her best friend Bianca
skipping to silly schoolgirl rhymes
i'm under the cherry tree
swollen ankles propped
on the little brick wall
soon Andrew will bring out espresso
with a touch of grappa
good for the digestion
we will talk into the night
wanting summer to last   forever

i want to remember this
next time i'm angry at life.

Sunday and You

take me there my love
by the brook
beneath the white clouds
knitted in the summer sky

there, by the dry arms
of our tree
where i felt my limbs multiply
and root themselves in you

there, where the jealous sun
watched our eyes fly out
and become poems

and the gentle leaves
embarrassed by our kisses
made a game of our lives

i want to lie by the hem
of the brook with you
eating the sounds
our hearts make
once more

Getting Things Right

i am
therefore
i make no apologies
woman
italian
overweight
underweight
tall   loud
romantic bore

i take no responsibility
for his broken heart
his buried body
the vacancies in his life
i accept the colour of my eyes
i will not blame my ancestors
for their darkness
i will not blame them
for my hunger for my desire
to devour the world around me
i am through
blaming the forces outside
my soul
it is unproductive

it is time you stopped
your war with my memory
making me the devil
in your desires
go on,   be the priest
you're a great liar.

The Old Man

a fireplace
an old wooden bench
potatoes buried
under hot ashes
an old man
chews tobacco
and tells stories
of a distant land
he discovered in letters

outside the trees
are furious with the wind

his hands tremble
too many years loving
the wheat in borrowed fields

his eyes are wet moons

too many tall sons
and slender daughters
have left shadows behind

somewhere in the night
crickets are clowning
and hot ashes are cooling

Il Vecchio

un focolare
un vecchio banco
di legno
patate coperte
da ceneri calde
un vecchio mastica tabacco
e racconta storie
di un paese lontano
scoperto in lettere

fuori gli alberi
sono furiosi col vento

le dita tremano
troppi anni amando il grano
di una terra prestata

i suoi occhi sono lune bagnate

troppi figli
sono ombre lasciate

nella notte grilli scherzano
e calde ceneri   rinfrescano

Beautiful Things

brave beautiful things
have their own shape
the belly at nine months
the winter maple in my backyard
in its January coat
the light above the photograph
of Gia at three months
they do not need words
                                        they are
the cemetery where my father
sleeps in winter, spring
forever

i walk down the perfect stone path
to the tall mausoleum
place flowers by his name
he lies on the sixth floor
overlooking the stillness
the numbness of peace

these flowers will breathe
the ice of this month
and they will be beautiful
in silence

i come and sit on the bench
visit with this man
i could never talk to
and have long conversations

For Gia at Bedtime

she smells of something so beautiful
it has no name
her face is the passion fruit flower
i held in my hands as a child
and never let go
she brings back all the evenings
of spring in the farmhouse
she gives her smile freely
without conditions
she loves the size of my belly.
i read her stories
in her room of painted giraffes
and clouds
she does not interrupt
i watch her stretch her long, thin arm
over her favourite blanket
and close her eyes.
i think of poems i might write
but there is no image for this moment
for who she is
my only daughter
my prayer
the greatest poem of my life.

from:

Daughters for Sale

Loreta, la Calda

they won't talk about sex
they talk about everything else

it embarrasses them
as if their children were all
announcements by Gabriel
you know   the angel

not me
it doesn't embarrass me
i had my legs wide open
as well as my eyes

look at their faces
they hide them
red with shame for having
desires

not me
i felt my man
and he felt me
i was so beautiful
non sapeva dove metterlo

you think i am vulgar
i talk vulgar
an old woman should not
talk so vulgar

but i wasn't always old
only death is old
only death is   vulgar

Daughters for Sale

for Rosaria

Re-entering the past is a dangerous adventure
—Elizabeth Smart

you want to listen to my story
how polite you are
but it will not make a difference

you will laugh a little
a little you will cry
it will not change anything

tears and laughter change nothing
i have done both   many times
even when i   believed
i am not a dreamer anymore

sit
i will tell you my story
because you say you want to hear it
but do not judge everything by me
stories   are all i have left.
i was born far from this perfect garden
of cement and wrought iron
i was born a fish in a Calabrian sea
i cannot remember the name
it was a Greek name
on the other side was Sicily

touch my skin
feel how rough, dry, like salt
sometimes i can taste my skin
it smells of the sea
i lift my face to feel the sun
i remember the way it walked
on my flesh
warm, soft like an angel and sometimes
with the fiery steps of the devil

in this garden the sun wears   shoes

i came here a long time ago
before your mother thought of you
it was after Mussolini took my mother's
gold wedding ring
and my brother
his dead body in her arms
his blood on the cobble stones of the piazza
the church bells   screamed
my father went crazy
he just walked about talking to nothing
talking to my brother
to the empty spot at the table
talking to the fireplace
until his tongue dropped   forever

not long after i married a man from
a photograph
a photograph sent from across the ocean
i married a man i recognized only
from the waist up
a man in an envelope

i prayed he had legs

the man was our passport
our ticket to   paradise
i did not know about paradise
was it farther than Naples?
the man had legs and he had arms
he gave me bread   i gave him children
he had very large hands
but not large enough to touch me

my man is gone
and my children are busy
so i sit here by this fountain
with all this wool in my hands
i knit

what do you think they will do
with all my knitting
when i am   done

The Last Confession

for Peppina

the only real sin
is   being born

my son sits in quiet duty
at the foot of my hospital bed
he has not removed his coat
he is not sure whether
to go or to stay
his legs are uncrossed

he took the day off work
to bring me here
his wife did not come
she did not want to lose
a day's pay
i understand the value of
a day's pay

my son is not my child   anymore
he cannot comfort me
i cannot comfort him
the years have changed our position
they say that is the way it should be

my daughter will come soon
to relieve him
he will go without guilt

i must look presentable
because my children care
i must comb my hair
and pass a wet face cloth
over my eyes and body

my daughter will force me to powder
my skin
she will rub cream on my brittle hands
straighten my bed
make sure i eat everything on my tray
she will insist i walk
so my blood will travel
to the parts of me i no longer feel

my body wants to rest
lie flat
my arms want to fold over my
sunken chest
and my eyes, my eyes want to
lose themselves deep into what
they have left of   memories

my children do not want me to die
death is much too final
like the dark after a sunset
it interrupts everything

my daughter tells me there will be visitors
so i must wear my best nightgown

i do not need visitors
what to say to a visitor about my pain
pray with me, eat an orange

will they understand
i do not have my language anymore
will they recognize   me
the fourth bed in this room
the old   quiet woman in the
new nightgown
in the corner by the window
a box of fine imported chocolates
on the night table

La Vacandin

for Esterina

my name is Esterina
but everyone calls me *La Vacandin*
because my belly is vacant
empty of children
i did not find a man to fill me

i live in my brother's house
a maid to his wife
my brother is dead now
and i am still here

a woman without children has no home
a woman without a man is always a guest
in her brother's house

Her Son

for Celestina

i watched her fuss over him
as if he were a prince
a divine gift from God
her golden child
with the clear glass eyes
and natural curls
a perfect little man with
perfect little parts

when he grew
i watched her caress his shirts
with her bent fingers
as she ironed out each crease
erasing any evidence of imperfection

i watched her fold each one
into a perfect square
buttoned to the neck
then she'd straighten the chest of drawers
and gently lay each piece of clothing
as if they were blessed

with the care and concentration
of the women in church who arranged
the altar

i watcher her prepare his lunch
the sandwiches always moist
the fruit unbruised

and always something she had baked
for his sweet tooth
then she'd slip the twenty-dollar bill
into his trouser pockets
just in case

when he allowed her
she would caress his strong cheeks
'*bello mio*' she would whisper
and then place her fingers on her lips
as if she had let slip some deep secret

he could do no wrong

i watched her stare out into
a thousand midnights
waiting
a soft shadow pinned to the lace curtain
waiting
for the lights of his car to silence her heart
his footsteps up the walk
his key in the door
and then she would   breathe
and disappear

i watched her love him
without   fatigue
without   expectations
then i would go and iron
my own clothes

The Bride's Return

for Antonietta

the red hot Sicilian sun
will not wait
one day is all he has left
silent
on his mother's best sheets
on the pale cotton blanket
she crocheted with the last
light of her eyes
the African breath from across the sea
will not allow much more time

the women in black
in the month of July
they sit around his still body
wailing in chorus
as quick fingers fondle the smooth
pebbles of rosary beads
the men   solemn
in their arm band and black buttons
stand like dark pillars
around the crowded room

the children's nervous laughter
spilling and scattering
like large stones in the hard
corners of the courtyard

his young bride is on a train
Rome to Sicily, 1948

it is a long, slow trip
the young bride has eyes
the colour of new walnuts
they settle over the countryside
and through sleepy lids they
glimpse the lazy summer hills
and the endless parade of
tall umbrella pines

she will meet the procession
when her journey ends
unaware
and swallow the thick scent
of chrysanthemums
gasp for air

she will remember   forever
the hot Sicilian sun with its
cruel   open grin

The Last Season

for Marisa

which season do i ask for
one more summer to plant the seeds
to watch my garden grow
to dig up the fig tree my father
left behind
to watch the sun drape itself
around the trees
the way my grandmother draped her
shawl around me
one more summer to watch my
children's changing bodies
their beautiful skin exposed

do i ask for autumn
i am fond of autumn
of the taste of crisp apples

how much time is enough time
the seasons are too short
and now my life is measured by
just one more

i am not ready to die
so i pray all the prayers i have learned
i kiss all the relics and cross myself
with holy water
i sleep with the pictures of saints
the with stigmata of *Padre Pio*
in my pillow case

my friends sit around me
talk of the past

they are here to help me
i accommodate them
they are sincere
but i want the   future
i want the seasons over and over
i want to be at my children's wedding
i am not afraid   God
i am just not ready

My Father's Cane

i sit on the cement stoop
below my father's black
and white photograph
the one he used the last time
for his passport
the date of his birth and death
in clear print
on a smoky, square marble
the white magnolia petals
scattered like giant communion wafers
on the soft waking earth
the birds do their silent dance
balancing on the gravestones
the trees wear their green
like a new haircut.
it is a magic afternoon
the kind we pray for
and hunger for each time
this season decides to
tease us again.
my father's cane beside me
it is what he left me
that is practical
i use it when my back
refuses to hold me
it accompanies me
when i visit
on special occasions
Christmas, Easter
when nostalgia and guilt
invade my heart.
i have little to say to him now

thirteen years since we ended
the argument
i no longer rely on the anger
i justified with youth
his cane in my hand
and i understand his steps
the weight of his legs
the wounds in his heart.
this place i come to
rarely
gives me back my father
the one i wanted in my life
the one who loved me
that way i wanted to be loved

perhaps it is the season
that forgives
that refuses to judge
i know here
beneath this blue sky
with my feet on the earth
i let the tears flow
without shame
without fear
i hear them being swallowed
deep into the white silence
of my father's bones
his dry bones
that have no more need
for his cane

Ladies of the Caravelle

the photographs
are all black and white
young olive-skinned women
with thick hair piled neatly
at the back of the neck
or cut short in tight curls

i recognize the coral beads
my grandmother wore four strings
of them around her neck
my older cousins were fortunate
in their inheritance
have fashioned the beads as earrings
pins and other decorative things

the smiles never reveal the teeth
they are smiles for photographs
hands poised on someone's shoulder
or the back of a chair

sometimes they are holding something
awkward
that seems not to belong
a pair of white lace gloves never worn
a crystal glass
a bouquet of perfect flowers

their skin is flawless   beautiful
beautiful with being young
beautiful with being photographed.
i sit with them on Saturday afternoons
the long table filled with home made
biscotti and *ciambelle*

they show me each photograph with
so much pride   excitement
and with each one there is a story
of a town
a man
a wedding
a death
and with each one there is a song
in dialect   i understand

we arrange the images on bristle board
label the year   the region   the date of
departure the port of escape
then the names   Maria, Concetta
Adele, Rina, Rosa   Speranza

they will be on display
in the lobby of a building
strangers will come to view them
interpret their beauty   history
their cultural significance

but strangers will not hear the song
in dialect
the women packaged that for me
to take home
with the leftover *biscotti*

Perfect Love

he left me for a girl
who drove a beige Subaru

he left me for a girl
whose breasts didn't need
a bra

he left me for a girl
whose smooth white thighs
opened   without guilt

he left me for a girl
who didn't need confession
who didn't hang rosary beads
on bedroom walls

he left me for a girl
whose blood was bluer
than her eyes

he left me for a girl
whose accent was charmingly
English

he left me for a love
that wouldn't confuse him
a love that was   perfect

she left him for someone
with a bigger   car

Donna/Woman

only when a woman is
nothing
but a dream he believes
when she walks on his heart
a ghost
who brings back his   identity
the history they stole
when they bundled him up
and took him away

only a dark woman without
voice
a dark woman whose eyes
are his
only when a woman is nothing
but a muse
a subject to write about
an angel   witch
whose poison he drinks
to remember   to be
to write
and when a woman is
only   this
can she be killed so easily
in the name of love

Cuore

i have taken my heart
to so many places
like Hansel and Gretel
in the dark of the forest
i left bits and pieces
pebbles of light
to find my way back
back
to my father's house
where the lamp is dim
but always lit
back to where my friends live
where there is always a chair
for me and a full glass of wine
back to re-arrange my clothes
my boxes of photographs
then again i take my heart
to the next place
where it is home for a while
a little less heavy than before
but alone   with itself
until that autumn afternoon
when the wind forced its way
into my open chest
and i stumbled into you
a pebble in a canyon
a seed in an endless field
just one single note
to complete the   symphony

i have taken my heart
to so many places   now
it will not move anywhere
without you

Ode to Balls

i could say his ego is the size
of Los Angeles
but that would be   kind
let me speak to you of his
genitals

he was always admiring his
in mirrors
shiny tiles on bathroom walls
even the toaster   when it was
strategically placed
i often moved the espresso pot
out of his way
they were everywhere
i bumped into them from
across the room
i found them in open drawers
lounging romantically
on the balcony floor
how he loved   them
he could not do enough for   them
wrote poems
played music for   them
John Denver records
he photographed them in colour
black and white
lit perfumed candles on summer nights
i believe he's left them everything
in his will
and on Saturday nights
he dressed them up
and took them dancing

how he loved them
they weren't fat
they weren't awkward
they weren't loud
they were   graceful
they danced into the room and
his world stopped

i could say his ego is the size of
Los Angeles
but that would be kind

I Might Have Been Sicilian

if her first husband had lived
i might have been   Sicilian
i might have learned to swim
in the blue waters of the Ionian
i might have been less tall
my hair a different shade
my dialect less   musical
i might have felt the *scirocco*
from Northern Africa
and climbed lemon trees
but he died while his young bride
spoke to her sisters about her new life
not in Canada but in *Catania*
he died while his bride
sat beneath the Roman pines
speaking of the gentle husband
who bought her dresses that
swung in perfect circles
he died while the accordion played
love songs to *Donna Rosa*
as she freed her braids to the summer moon

if he had lived long enough
to give her children
i might have been   Sicilian

A Mother Poem

I

mamma had no time to baby me
after her breasts emptied and my
father packed his one suitcase
crossed the ocean to prepare a new life
for all of us
he hung his blue jacket on the nail
by the kitchen door
left it behind, the pockets empty
of chocolates

mamma took a job at the local hospital
long hours, midnight shifts, Sundays
she held the hands of the dying old
wiped the blood of premature mothers
boiled the instruments
learned to give advice
and every other afternoon she would bike
for miles from town to town injecting needles
to the *contadini*

mamma had no time for playgrounds
she left me in the catholic arms
of Sister *Bernarda* and Sister *Plaudilla*
whose small dry breasts were resting places
for large crucifixes
no room there for small faces with wet eyes

mamma thought i was in good hands
safe hands
what better hands than those of the sacred
the divine
she knew nothing of the darkness of the
Medieval Tower
she only ever saw the large *portone*
the waiting room where the nuns brought
me down to visit
all starched and combed

mamma fed me *ricotta* and *maretozzi*
and in between kisses i could hear
her heart
i could feel her body shake each time
she put her arms around me to
whisper good-bye
but my screams didn't convince her
to turn back
i watched her walk away toward the hospital
her sky blue sweater on her shoulders
her tight curls stiff as her footsteps
mamma never turned around

II

my baby wears Nikes
and little Gap shirts
she is full of authors and magic
music and Raffi
she loves the park and Canada's Wonderland
i'm my baby's personal driver
i'm her immediate cash drawer
sometimes she remembers i'm there
"i love you mommy, can we go to McDonalds?"

III

when i was eight Sister *Bernarda*
made me a pallbearer
a little white casket on six little shoulders
our steps controlled and careful
over the cobblestones

IV

my baby is scared of ghosts
only wants stories with happy endings
sometimes i read a story with a
different ending … it makes her cry
then my baby looks like   me

mamma takes her in her arms
fills her with kisses and chocolate bars
trying to buy back a little bit of   time
mamma cannot bear to hear her cry
and when my baby calls her name
mamma always turns around.

Winters

how short the winters have become
January is no longer the   enemy
this season she dreaded
like the magnolia dreads that cruel
breath of wind
this season is so much tamer now
she fools herself into thinking the years
are kinder
time moves so much faster   now
too fast to linger long in the dream
to dine slowly
she has put away the fur coat
it is not needed or   correct
no time to clean out the summer closet
all seasons fit in harmony with each
other's dust
even the birds outside her window
refuse to fly away
they make do on the stale bread
the snow melts   quickly

My Husband

sometimes i think my husband
is a saint   he allowed himself
to be re-baptized just to marry me
he let the priest do that holy water thing
all over his New Zealand Anglican head
he became Catholic
just to marry me
took the sacred vows wore a suit and tie
danced with my aunts
just for   me
the girl with the wrong package
the most unlikely debutante
but my husband is a   silent saint
polite   discreet
unlike the saints i grew up with
who held their eyes in their hands
paraded their open wounds
bled openly for admiration   canonization
my husband is a sort of socialist saint
understated
he carries his heart not on his sleeve
but neatly tucked into his breast pocket
keeping mine company

from:

Ciao Baby

Simple Heart

i will not write epics
to anthologize
sometimes ideas hurt my head
they take me places where
i am not comfortable
where i am always a stranger

but i will write about   you
the gentleness you are
inside my arms
the scent you bring
with your morning eyes
all the possibilities
there in the almond shapes
beneath your brows

i will write about the treasure
you are in your dollar t-shirt
your hand me down jeans
you make all the ideas take a
second seat
there is too much of me you want
too much of me you need
and i am yours
i will find my dreams again
because of you
my tender string bean
who grows so tall   so quickly

i must keep the muscles moving
must exercise the knees
keep on walking to meet you
halfway wherever we are going

take my hand   my heart
they have been yours from
the first breath
they will be yours long after
the ideas have been explored

My English Love

that i am loved at all   surprises me
that i am loved by you   mystifies me

but it is twenty years from that
summer night beneath a Sunday moon
on holiday
fat and golden against a huge Canadian sky

such a foreign face   such a timid smile
good evening never sounded so musical
that you stood as i began to sit
was charming
that you spoke my name
Giovanna   without mistake
and suddenly it was the right name
each vowel and consonant   perfect
it was always the right name
waiting for the sound you were

my heart began to re-arrange its history
making room for you

that i have not written you love poems
in twenty years is a   mystery
but perhaps poets only write about
what is missing

Five Small Lives

she has dried the tomatoes
in the Canadian sun
it takes a little longer
but they are red and sweet
on the tongue
she has blanched the green beans
bushels of them
stored them in clear jars
with mint, garlic and oil
the house is giddy
with the wonderful smells
the mouth waiting watering
ready for the tastes only she
can provide
she has labelled each jar
with her name   and date
each letter perfectly curled
and slanted
her first and last name in
permanent black marker
the name she learned to write
just to label her jars

*

the sidewalks are made of cement
he understands cement
the way academics understand
the meaning of things beyond
what the words tell
he knows the amount of water
the necessary time for shaping
smoothing and setting

his hands are the size of his
work shoes
he cannot talk about much
blaming the language
the scarcity of time for knowledge
but when he talks cement
what an articulate tongue

*

Maria's bones are making her shorter
so she combs her hair just a little higher
she is dreaming of   freedom
from children and schools
dreaming of Paris and London
maybe a summer in Tuscany
with roses and edible greens
Germaine Greer lives in Tuscany
perhaps they will exchange
gardening tips
but Maria is not a gardener
she is the eldest daughter
the unmarried one
the one who lives with her
mother

*

the desk is still full
with things she belonged to
the pencil case with the
butterfly stickers
the pre-teen magazines
the girls all shared
the sharpened pencil crayons
neon markers and a word puzzle

that wasn't complete
she struggled with the English words
but they would soon be mastered
the slightly scuffed running shoes
with the Barbie image on the side
were the new culture she was
learning to wear

the desk is still full
it will stay untouched
for the remainder of the term
receiving unspoken questions
of her classmates
why their friend was thrown
out of a balcony window
like a baseball
in the hands of a mad tortured man
who had one last statement to make

*

Old man Joe walks his dog
in the school yard across the laneway
each night about 9:15
the signs are there   NO DOGS ALLOWED
but he's learned to ignore
much more than signs so he stands
by the fence and lets Carbone the dog
run free
when he whistles the dog comes running back

black as coal that dog is
black as night itself
unless the moon is full
you can only feel his movements

i've stopped on occasion
exchanged some words in italian
his thick accent from a dialect
born in a small town he can no
longer remember
he calls me *signora*
there is respect in that word
in the way he delivers it

i am a new immigrant in comparison
he has been here since 1949

where is the America of my grandfathers?
he asks
no longer here for sure
he answers
we left them the America
we made room left them lots of room
the ones who stayed behind
are comfortable
they sit in their own sunshine
collect government cheques
bank the money we send
argue with their children
in a language they both understand
but here in this America
we must keep moving not time to
sit in the sunshine
no time to walk the dog in the daytime
but i am lucky
at least my dog has no need for language
he understands my whistle

buona sera Signora
buona sera

Two Fat Girls

in the 1970's
we walked St. Clair Avenue
from Dufferin to Lansdowne
as if it was our home town
as if we owned it
the wide Avenue with large sidewalks
spilling with other *paesani* who had
also claimed it theirs

grocery stores crammed with delicacies
from Sicily and Calabria
from Molise to Lazio
artichokes, eggplants shiny trophies
on the sunny open market

Tre Mari Bakery where we stopped for
zeppole on the feast of St. Joseph
and that one treasured café
where we spent our street life
sipping cappuccino before they were cool

maybe we were just two fat girls
maybe we were just two stupid girls
romantic and silly
just two young girls

i remember you wanted a husband
and i wanted just to be loved
and neither one of us knew
where to find what we were looking for
so we walked the Avenue
in our three inch heels

like models on a runway
with our skirts split at the back
our strong, young legs teasing
such innocence
you with your perfect breasts
and me the tall one
swinging our purses
to the rhythm of our hips
just past *Tricolore* Pool Hall
where the young immigrant studs
cigarettes in hand
whistled and lusted
"hey Susie baby, sleep with me tonight"
but we were just two fat girls
dark haired and free
laughing out loud
as we paraded by
because we knew they could
only have us with their   eyes

My Nephew

my brand new nephew and i
our noses glued to the bay window
in the new house
in the new subdivision
watching the flashing light
on the Wonderland Mountain
my little Gatsby
mysterious little man
was there ever a time before   you
before your smile
that floods my mother's eyes
before your needs
so selfish and immediate
before your arms so impulsive
your tiny hand on my shoulder
your cheek caressing mine
we watch the sky light up
with magic fireworks
a storm of invading fireflies
your breath steady and warm
against my face
i am prepared to give you anything
anything
for the price of your smile

Notes on Aging

I am a woman, and dusty, standing among new affairs.
I am a woman who hurries through my prayers.
—Gwendolyn Brooks

i am middle aged now
something i thought would
only happen to others
has happened to me

*

i sometimes think
i have been old all my life
Italian women are born old
they carry the weight
right from the womb
old with fear
old with responsibility
the first beat of the heart
pounding out fear
like an eleventh commandment

*

lately it seems all words are about
loss
always about leaving
what to write about my life
always in the past
the days become history quickly
i cannot write the future

*

i am lost without dreams
when did they stop
such a dreamer i was
such fantasies   possibilities
but all around me there is
pain
dreams have stopped
the flicker of a candlelight
out with a quick breath
no warning
even my pen is heavy to lift

*

i am looking for a reason to
write about snow
looking for a muse in the cracks
of my life
looking for a landscape to tickle
the heart
but i am sad
my steps are timid in the
winter night   awkward
i miss running
miss the laughter in my mother's house
where she lives alone
miss the length of my hair
its black sheen
i miss my father's   anger
strange this aging

*

i will leave my poems somewhere
in time they will be stumbled upon

and my father's name will live on
without sons

*

i want to write about my dying aunt
i hate the word   dying
she isn't dead yet
why should i think that death
will be her next visitor
but the blood clots and many
throughout her lungs
her arms and legs no longer move
her chest heaves   painfully
with each breath
i bend to kiss her brow
her skin smells clean sweet with
talcum powder
i caress the sparse white curls
lift her still hand
pray for that miracle
but miracles do not happen
to old women
in Scarborough hospitals
in cold Canadian winters

*

i am nothing
she is nothing
we are nothing
but a breath
a moment
a sunrise
a storm
a silence

*

she asks if my husband is well
if my child has grown tall and strong
go home   she says
the weather is bad and the road long
between home and   here

*

a slow tearing in my heart
a last love letter
another wound to heal
soon another gravestone
to visit
another voice in my life
silenced

*

forty years
eighty years
a long time   a short time
when is death less tragic
it is life we lose each time
we are less

*

in my culture
middle aged poets are not
highly regarded
unlike doctors or lawyers
and   land developers
poets

hold no position of value
you cannot measure
their worth in   real estate

*

my aunt will never know
i write poems for her
her life without metaphors
lived with the rhythm of a broken language
thirty years spent in airless factories
my dying aunt will not read my poems
but i know her life helped me
write them

*

my heart is strong
my mother's lineage
in my father's family the hearts
were weak   took them early
my aunt hangs on
that muscle broken over and over
with time   will not give up
women's hearts grow stronger
with each rupture
maybe
women's hearts never die
my aunt
my mother   my sister
my nieces   my daughter
me
one heart   forever strong
infinite

Good Friday, The Passion

the magnolia is resisting
the final winter slap
each year it struggles towards
another resurrection
each year i check the calendar
hoping for a premature re-birth

i want life again
in colour and perfume
i want the heat again in
white blinding sunshine
i want to stand at the corner
of Grace and Mansfield Avenue
on Good Friday
as the procession
makes its way unhurried
through the less catered streets
of my trendy neighbourhood

i want the sun to laugh at me
because the solemn faces
of my ancestors do not laugh
on such an occasion
they carry the cross
with reverence and apology

i am faithful
i attend each year
hoping i have grown
so sophisticated
i will finally carry
a video camera to record

the ethnic flavour
hoping i have grown
so liberated
i will sit at the *Diplomatico Café*
and laugh out loud
at the colourful spectacle
the way the new tourists do
enjoying life as theater

but i am taken in each time
by the haunting voices
of women chanting the rosary
by the somber tune
of the one hymn i recognize
i am taken in each time
by the beautiful young girls
at their mother's arms
by the old men
who move like my grandfather
their slow steps
in tune with a trumpet

i am the lost daughter of nostalgia
but my heart is not saddened by this
and i will be here again
in the sunshine or in the rain
as Jesus falls one more time
in the streets of my neighbourhood
knowing that even   i
will be somebody's history
somewhere along the line

The Other Woman

when the Virgin Mary is the other woman
you can kiss your lover's heart good-bye

when the Virgin Mary is the ideal mother
you have lost the argument with your son

when the Virgin Mary is the ideal   woman
no lipstick will ever be the perfect shade

you are no   competition

you are just a   woman
with a mountain of faults
just flesh and blood   hormones
that are misunderstood
a woman too difficult to console

so you can love them both till your
heart breaks
you can pray all the prayers
ever written
summon each blessed saint
for help and intervention
cry all the tears of this evil world

you will never be   salvation

you have bled in pain given life
lost your temper at times
even part of your mind   on occasion
you have taken pills for comfort
a cigarette or two

you have ironed enough shirts
to dress a planet

you are human   pure and simple

maybe it is time you lifted yourself
from that bed of wounds
learned to love yourself a little

because the other woman
sometimes   wins

Second Language

each language i speak
is a second language

there is a dialect
i understand my mother by

there are words i write
in English that my husband edits

there is a sound in my head
that sings my grandmother's songs

there is a language my heart speaks
that even i cannot translate

but language is always an issue
and i want to give you a voice
such a voice to be envied
spoken without error
nouns and verbs in the proper place
they will be stunned the strangeness
of it all....with the perfection of it all
your tongue unleashed like a wild
tango *erotico*

and you will give me your hands
with all their imperfections
open and waiting
and i will read in them
the stories and poems

we will trade souls for a while
you will give me
the reason for listening
for time and remembering
i will tear a sheet
of clean fresh paper from my head
free to write   a language
that is first second and last
a language our spirit
will understand

Figli Canadesi

chissà
se qualche volta pensano a noi
due o tre generazioni   di noi
ormai ripiantati
cresciuti e sbocciati
in nuovi colori
tra i giardini di Toronto
Woodbridge e Bolton
tra i nuovi castelli di
King City

chissà
se qualche volta pensano
alle nostre ragioni
giuste ed ingiuste
al calcio in culo
chissà
se l'università offre dei corsi

Chi Siamo?
Chi Eravamo?
quanti figli cacciati da casa
quanti orfani delusi
certi di noi ancora   cittadini
per memoria   per nostalgia
fors anche   per dispetto

Picasso had Paris

Picasso had Paris
and Gertrude Stein's living room
where they all came for
scotch and conversation
Picasso had Paris like a beautiful
mistress
a forgivable sin
he had the soul of his lover
and not just the sex
had the night with all its temptations
smoke filled cafes where life
clung thick and scented then
exploded fireworks over the Seine

Pasolini had Rome and its
mysterious fountains
the dark side of the moon
behind the *Cuppolas*
he had the angels he loved
and the demons he fought
and Rome and the night had his
heart

i have Clinton and College
on a January night
with a skinny cappuccino
and a DuMaurier light

Ena and the Sleeping Giant

in the Havelock Hills of Hawkes Bay
sleeps a giant   the *Maori* legend tells
an enormous giant spread out beneath
the land of the long white cloud
a country i fell in love with
when the man i love took my hand
and introduced me to the playgrounds
of his childhood landscapes
a land of sea and hills

he brought me home to a new family
i belonged to   instantly
to the garden on Greenwood Road
where Ena sat each afternoon
on the wooden bench beneath
her open bedroom window
and with a voice that soothed
the weight of my journey
she shared the magic of her
New Zealand garden
the Latin and English name of every
flower   every plant
new and strange to my city girl heart
except for the rose and the passion flower
i recognized from a time in another garden
where my grandmother prayed on her knees

Ena offered me tea by the persimmon tree
fat with orange fruit   a feast for the birds

Ena knew me by my foreign name *Giovanna*
i knew her by her gentle touch her voice
her elegant hands
her short bread cookies on the silver tray
hydrangea arranged in the proper vase
sipping sunlight slowly like her
five o'clock sherry

there is a giant asleep on the hills
of Havelock North
in a land where my husband's mother
walks   forever
among the gardens that have no rival
where the rose and the passion fruit
grow beautiful and   quiet

I Wish I Were a Poet

i wish i were a poet   he said
so i could write about it

that your body became light
weightless
after the final turn to its side
not by your own muscles
but by the hands of a stranger
paid to move you

he would have wanted to be there
to be those hands
who would move your resigned flesh
to its comfortable side
to understand your last pain
your last pleasure
to understand the final breath

would he have seen your soul rise
from you   what shape
what intoxicating scent it might bring
perhaps of your beloved roses
but he is here   a thousand miles away
in a pale green kitchen without roses
thinking of you as tears mix with the
scent of strong coffee
wishing he had the power of metaphors
so he would never lose you

One More Time

my love affair with Italy is coming
to an end the passion smoldering
a small spark that sometimes ignites
but quickly cools

all affairs have their time

but on winter nights in this land
of snow
when i fall into drawers straightening
the past into neat folded piles
i come across your photograph
your arm in mine solid secure
your short stained pants and awkward smile
under that September tree
and i can almost taste the figs you brought me
wrapped in their own dark leaves
i can hear your voice across the field
clear as a bell
and that little boy kiss you planted
forever in my heart and i think
maybe i would like to fall in love again
one more time

We Are The Good Children

we are the good children   so successful
we have built *villas*
for the surviving parents
landscaped the gardens with exotic plants
added statues of angels
scattered them as trophies of granite and marble
among the thorns of trimmed rose bushes

we have smoothed down the *bocce* courts
with fine red clay   lined them with
comfortable benches made of cedar
and Canadian maple
the mandatory fountain in the middle
of the garden pissing away its wet
song of nostalgia

we are the good children   so successful
we hold charity balls where we dress
in Armani, Versace and Klein
the women all perfectly waxed
the men all perfectly groomed
we are beautiful   we are special
we parade our visibility and celebrate

all in honour of mothers and fathers
before us
of those who could not make themselves
comfortable in the hearts of children-in-law
for those who simply got too old

we are the good children   grown so sophisticated
so modern so quickly   independent

but we have not forgotten their sacrifices
our pockets full of money
the down payments made on our homes
the children they   raised
while we were busy with the building
the adopted   dream

now we build villas   landscaped *villas*
without grandchildren

we visit on Sundays bringing fruit
and photographs
help feed the birds for an hour or two
keeping an eye on the slow moving
imported   clock

Ciao, Baby!

it was summer
the hills were green
moss gone sour
the sun hid behind them   like
a child between the safe folds
of a mother's skirt
the oak tree was full
a giant umbrella
your bare feet dangled among the
fat leaves   i looked up
you hit me with the acorns
turned your reckless hair toward the sky
i called you   again and again
begged you to come down
held out my hand to trade one last walnut
one last shiny marble   you hit me again
and let me leave   with the back of your head
i left for my great adventure   without you
on a ship named   Augustus
and you didn't even say
"ciao baby"

St. Joseph's Girls

in 1967 dressed in my navy blue
wool uniform with a black bow tie
a blazer and sensible oxford shoes
i took the bus from Lansdowne and
St. Clair to the Bloor subway station

stood for the nine stops to Sherbourne
i was a big girl in grade nine
in the Centennial year   all on my own
crossing the big, big city for my future

*

St. Joe's Commercial High School
was just a small school
nearly three hundred immigrant girls
some light   some dark some big
some small and   me   i was tall

*

just across the street from St. Joe's
was the Selby Hotel   seedy and sinful
where Hemingway hung out in his days
when Toronto was his hangout
the nuns warned us about the Selby
it was no place for St. Joseph's girls
so we only thought about it

*

Sister Laura Ann taught us typing
on the old Underwood typewriters

j-u-j space k-i-k space

the rhythm of her pointer stick
on the desk and ledge
our obedient fingers hit the letters
the thumb caressed the space bar

she taught us Pitman shorthand
as if it were a secret language
one that would reveal our lives
the lives of girls like me
to be shaped and moulded into fine
secretaries

d-e-d space l-o-l space

but i could not write poetry in
Pitman shorthand
so i left

from:

What My Arms Can Carry

What My Arms Can Carry

how do i package
the weight of my heart

i will take with me
what my heart can carry

a suitcase
a handful of photographs
the cotton shawls
my grandmother crocheted
with the dimming light
of her dark blue eyes

i will take with me
my grandfather's watch
on the silver chain
the carved wooden handle
of his bent cane
these things
i will honour
in a special place
in my new home

these things will remind me
of who i am
and where i came from

but who i am is many things

i am a name and a landscape
a language and a dialect
i am memory and history
the present and the future

i am the children i will bear
the man and woman
who will survive

i will take with me
what my arms can carry

Street of Widows

for mamma

they live alone
in their own house
paid for
free of mortgage
they will not leave quietly
for anyone's convenience
not their own children
not their children-in-law

they will be carried out
one or two will fall victim
to the disintegration
of muscle and bone
the others will be victims
of time

but for now
it is their street
the street of widows
where my mother lives
where she visits the others
whose husbands are more
recent losses

they prepare tables
with crisp cotton tablecloths
fill them with all the talent
from their individual hands
they feed each other

stories and food
the occasional glass of red wine
then they laugh till sleep comes

they are strong with each other
understand everything without
extra words
they connect arms
into an unbreakable chain
and take evening walks
to the local church
where God waits
a little reluctant
and then
an ice cream
on their way home

My Mother Wants

my mother is a practical woman
she wants nothing more
than my complete happiness

nothing more than to hear
my voice each day
free of anxiety or pain

nothing more than to know
my heart is strong and
full of love

she births me again
with every heartbeat

it is this unbelievable need
to love me with every molecule
that keeps her breathing

she needs nothing more
than my dreams, my ambitions
to know success

my mother wants only my truth
never acknowledging the lies
between us they are non-existent

i am completely at home
in her love

there is no country or flag
no discourse on belonging
that must allow birth a definition

it is pure love that makes it home

i too am a practical woman
i want nothing more than
my mother to live
forever

The Neighbourhood is Changing

the old men
have nowhere to go
banished, corroded barges
in some abandoned port
they sit
cooled by the winds of
passing streetcars
at the corner of Grace Street
and College

the faded wooden benches
are the only welcoming seats
that accommodate their time
so much time now
since their backs gave out
and their legs have jelly in them
since the pool halls became cafés

some see the world clearly
others through the pearly veils
of fallen cataracts
but their conversations are loud
and lucid
still the passion in their voices
in the stories they pitch
to each other
in the need to be heard

the old men sit
and the old women walk
the length of Grace Street

to the grand doors of St. Francis
each morning at eight
the doors open to prayers
to the lighting of candles
the necessary confessions
the blessing of the Eucharist

i make my way
in the neighbourhood
school bag in hand
the old men tip their hats
and offer a greeting

buon giorno, signora

i have time for a smile
a few words about the weather
the impending arthritis
the change in the neighbourhood
then i am off
to the sound of a bell
to fill the needs of my students

i will see them again
on my way home
heavy with the day's stress
and obligations
they are still there
waiting for the sun
to retire

sometimes i am aware there is
one old man less
one less story to pitch
one less voice to greet my mornings

one less hat tipped to existence

sì, *il quartiere sta cambiando*

A Song for Saro

you called me Giannissima
as if my birth name
was not large enough
to embrace all i appeared to be
inside your eyes

i was just a girl
a girl ripe for heartache
just another girl
in the little black book
and the little black heart
of your roommate

i was the girl who listened
to your guitar
and understood the songs
you wailed out in dialect
a dialect your own lover
found primitive

but it was she
who lay next to you
and loved your primitive soul
it was she
who sent you to heaven
and back

until love became too confusing
and dialects began dying
another immigrant boy
rides the sky tonight
with a mouth full of poems
in search of paradise

Perché Ti Amo

tu sei il sole di mezzogiorno
on my flesh
on a July afternoon
beneath the poplars
overlooking Georgian Bay
you are the cotton sheets
cool on my skin
the sweet taste of tonic
with lime and gin

your arms are what i fall into
i travel the length of you
with an appetite
the solid
fragrant island that you are
splendid
my island

Woman Behind the Wall

punish me with death
all sins, all mistakes
all rights and wrongs
into the same dark hole

i am the woman
disappeared with her sins
and her glories
four months behind a wall
while my son cried himself to sleep
my mother prayed herself into limbo

punish me again
for trusting
for falling in and out of love
for falling into a mistake

withdraw me in silence
erase me quickly
because you are sure
that i have sinned

what do you know about sin
about my sins
as weak as we are
less than our dreams
living always in the warmth
the greenhouse of needs
a woman made flesh
a woman trusting her heart

i am here behind a wall

Saint Joseph

did my father ever hold me
in his arms with so much love
with so much patience

how gentle you are Joseph
as you hold your woman's child

Joseph with the white lily
and the pure heart
with the trim brown beard
and timid smile
patron saint of families
father of all fathers
carpenter and man

silent Joseph
i cannot think of any words
you have ever spoken
only your presence
strong and secure

my eyes will not move from you
in this church
where you stand dry and cold
in the darkest corner
barren of sunlight
only the dim flicker of an electric
candle

is it this church that inspires
me to cry
this church where my father

stood next to me
my little girl's body in a communion
dress of pure white polyester
my head adorned with lace and
plastic pearls
my father had no lily
he had no beard
he was an ordinary man
in a gray suit and a thin blue tie
my father and me
his arms stiff against his chest
my bride's dress starched against
my nervous knees

was he proud of me Joseph
as you are proud of your
woman's child

Mothers and Breasts

Trees are never felled … in summer … Not
when the fruit
… is yet to be borne
—Nikki Giovanni

all too suddenly
my baby
has developed breasts

young woman's breasts

all too suddenly
there is the obsession
of breasts

the shape
the size
the need for the perfect bra
the exact colour
the exclusive material
the comparison
the competition
the design beneath the t-shirt
the desired illusion
in the three-way mirror

at fourteen
there is the need to hide
everything from me

the nipples behind the towel
the distance of her desires
the whispered words
don't look mom

as if i had no breasts of my own
as if i had never seen
her tender body
scrubbed her clean
powdered every centimeter
of who she is
held her warm and fragrant
in my arms

my baby pushes away
the need for me
with such delicacy
and precision

hiding her belly button
her spindly legs
too long to have yet
developed shape
her angel face
too young to bear history
too sweet to begin
tasting the bitterness of
time

i remember my fourteenth year
differently
wanting my mother desperately
wanting the questions
the interest
wanting answers and more

my mother was too tired
too catholic
too sad
to recognize my needs

i vowed to be different
it is not always about choice
not always about what is correct
not always the right time

perhaps when she is fifteen
perhaps when i am fifty-one

The Dandelion

for Karen

the first dandelion
has bravely shaken
its bright yellow head
in your abandoned garden

i watch it stretch toward the sun
from my porch window
high above the aging cherry
it is the twenty second Spring
in my house
it would have been the sixteenth
in yours

i am continually amazed
at the re-birth
terrified that each winter
will slice the roots forever
and it is the end

but the dandelion persists
it brings back my grandmother
in her bright cotton scarves
the sharp little knife in her hand
digging out the deep roots
shaking off the soil
filling the sack
with our evening meal

i think where you might have been
when i helped grandma dress the
green jagged leaves with oil and vinegar

were you tying their golden heads together
a yellow bouquet for your grandmother

two lifetimes beneath two far away moons
half a century
and we are just two women
who have watched a garden grow
two women who have loved
each other's children
tending their games
watching them take shape

how enchanting
the view
how amazing
a tiny
bitter weed

Maggie/Peggie

i dream i am Margaret Atwood
not a nightmare at all

i love my new silhouette
my small feet in penny loafers
pallid, clear skin
my Canadian skin
my Canadian heart
beating to a less chaotic drum

no more Neapolitan songs
weeping and tragic
no more De Sica and Magnani
this small immigrant life
this woman unknown

gone is my life in black and white
the black of death
mourning ancestors through
reminiscence and longing
the white of an unfamiliar landscape
indifferent and cold

no more misunderstanding identity
letting the passion loose
a mortal sin
devouring the language of too many vowels
where names are unpronounceable
unreadable

the displacement is gone
the loss
the numbness of invisibility

i am Margaret
i love my manicured hands
delicate
the perfection of my smile
the clarity of my name
the gentle
perfectly audible
perfectly edible
                                  voice

The Women I Am

i have grown large with the women
i am   heavy with passions and needs

mirrors inhabit my faces   each one
with something i recognize
my grandmother's eyes
my mother's nose
my sister's smile
each voice   different
demanding to be heard
each heart craving a love of its own

i am a woman invaded

i make you cry
but your tears are no longer
moved by my beauty
my skin   the length of my hair
your tears are for the   other woman
the woman of anger
whose desires are too great
for you to provide
she lives the heart of   regret
of dreams not met
of places not seen
the woman who hides deep
in the lunatic pocket of a   full moon

i make you laugh
and it is another woman still
the one you once caressed
on a summer night

in the month of August
foolish heart wanting laughter
promising youth   love
forever

reckless dreamer
living between words and punctuation
beneath lines and linens in hope chests
in flower pots and photographs

you love me   and i am the best
of women
soft   free of pain   darkness gone
my face without lines
my lips red and inviting

i am what you want to hold
the woman you wish would always be
home
to divide the minutes of the day
the hours and weeks that swell
into years

i come back with shadows
the smoke of a smoldering fire
and only the memory of warmth
light   a safe place
a room with curtains and soft chairs
Modigliani prints on a jonny-cake wall
long necked women with heavy heads
and thin eyes
and so many   appetites

Sempre

he looks at me
they are the same eyes
watching my hand
pass the brush
through my wet
less opulent dark hair
shaking my head
to loosen the curls

on the second floor balcony
of the *Auberge Charlobois*
my overgrown mass against
a white wall in a building
pretending to be Spanish

he speaks and his voice
still carries the slight accent
of his New Zealand roots

how many times have i watched
you comb your hair
on hot summer evenings

he takes me back
to the *Villa Rosa*
in *Siracusa*
to the white Sicilian sand
to wine sweet as vermouth
to prickly pears on cactus plants

back to the small
rented house carved into a hill
in *Piemonte*
back to Robin's terrace
overlooking Wellington's
Oriental Bay

the brush moves easily
through my thoughts
he has loved me perfectly
for so long
even the loss of my hair
does not disturb him

On a Country Road

the sky promises sunshine
you and i
in my little blue Honda
driving towards it
breaking off pieces
for our pockets

sitting beside you
i understand your breathing
i know   i am home

my mouth opens
there are things
i could interrupt
you with
but they will wait

this moment is
for my heart
pushing its way
into my eyes
beating
                    burning
at the sight of you

The Anniversary, Nov. 16

eighteen years,   papa
and it is yesterday
all days all years
memory
            softening

there are flowers still
rooted to the earth
a handful of tables
outside our favourite café
this November is spilling
with unusual   sunshine

your last day was much colder
dusted with the first snow
colours well hidden
the world wanting an early nap

tonight after visiting you
i am alone
a rare thing these days
the job
the children
the house
the husband
the poems
                        mamma

you would not believe
how much of me i   share
did you know me well   papa
did you hide it carefully

i am sitting at the last
table of two by the window
looking out at the intersection
of Clinton and College
you knew this corner well

i'm drinking a glass of wine
instead of coffee
New Zealand Sauvignon Blanc
how sophisticated your daughter
has become

always a pen in hand
ready to speak to   silence
the way i now speak to you
not needing the presence of flesh
or friend

i can sit
i can order a meal
i can order wine
without fear of being embarrassed
being a woman   alone

i am all grown up   papa
i can be me   all by myself
i can talk to you without anger
you would be proud

Marzo 21/2003

forty one years away
this spring day in my birth town
in this peninsula of dreams
and memories
loved by so many princes
paupers and fascists

i am another immigrant
you have heard it all   before
another torn and broken soul
forever in a storm
two moons
two hearts
two deaths.
today is San Benedetto
the first day of spring
birds perched on the railing
that lines the river
i sit by the statue of Padre Pio
fresh daffodils and mimosa
in a plastic vase

i look up at my cousin's building
above the town square
it is washed with the morning sun
her crisp laundry hanging from the balcony
the colourful flag of peace
bright in its stripes of purple and yellow
waves in the breeze.
the Bar Cavour is crowded
with gentlemen who no longer
need to be anywhere at a specific time

they drink coffee linger   talk of the
imminent war
Iraq and Iran
Saddam and Bush
and America   America
still the elusive America
like an old song on their lips
no mention of Canada

'you come from America'
they ask
i answer   no
i come from here
America is where i live.
i walk the tight winding streets
recalling the games
the skipping of cobblestones
savouring the smells from open windows
the songs on the radios
the faces of old women
their spent bodies on straw chairs
hands still busy with cottons and wool

i shall leave this town   soon
return to where i live   Canada
always a little fatter
and a little sadder

Bella

per Sophia

the English poet once wrote

truth is beauty
beauty is truth

that i shall search for this
all my life
to understand the meaning
of the words
simple as they appear to be

if it should live in a smile
that unburdens the ordinary day
and makes it lighter to carry

if it should be in the colour of her skin
the earth offering the scent
of spring lilies fresh from the rain
if i should find it in her walk
the gentle movement of her hips
in her eyes that tell a story you believe
completely
as you watch her hands stretch
over the blanket   removing the creases
till the bed is an altar you cherish

and when you sit in her presence
in comfort   without the need to go
and attend to other things

you look at her
and your heart says

è *bella,* è *veramente bella*

you know she is real
it is the truth of her
you discover

Ceprano/Carnevale

tomorrow the Lenten season begins
forty days of renewal
and sacrifice
a time to dust off the soul
revive the heart

it is *carnevale* and this town
is ready to party today
i stand back and watch the *piazza* ignite
costumes   music   laughter
children's joyful cries

i am a tourist   now
in this town i once called   home
this place i keep coming back to
looking for whatever it is i might
have left behind

it is not my town anymore
home is not about material
or cobblestones in a *piazza*
it is not the church or the bells
that ring each hour or the taste of
persimmons in late Autumn
although the cypress trees and umbrella pines
by the cemetery   always make me feel
at home

the bridge over the river is less impressive
than it once was
the sour smell of centuries
in the walls of abandoned buildings

the rubble   stains and litter
left to rot

my grandfather's house sold
long before my return
but the March sun is warm on my face
i watch the children dance
in the town square
oblivious to time   or history
it is all real and   unreal

the old men and old women
uncomfortable with age
holding on to stronger arms
leaning on canes
searching for an empty bench

their eyes sometime land on my
lumbering presence
and i wonder if somewhere
in their memory they might
recognize the child i once was
the one who once belonged here

but it is not home i return to
again and again
i am simply a stray cat
bewitched by   memory and
curiosity

Ritorno

i have come back to the house
where i was born
but it is only the road i recognize
long   winding beneath a bridge
the smell of new grass
the yellow mimosa in March
welcome me

the oak tree we climbed is gone
flattened into a driveway
the faded walls of a small house
revived by a bright melon yellow
no more rosemary bushes
or grapevine

the house belongs to a cousin now
his wife is polite
offers me coffee in porcelain cups

we sit beneath her new covered veranda
the red clay *canali* patterned into waves

there is insignificant chatter between us
we are strangers
she is in her fortieth year and pregnant
with her third child
i am here   unaccompanied

she escorts me to the bedroom
where i was born
i walk in alone   to an old woman
propped in the single bed
a loud television keeping her company

i move towards her
my feet argue each step
she turns and her curious gaze
suggests she is aware i must be
a relative

ciao zia

i tell her my name
she remembers i am her dead brother's
child

she offers her hand
it is small
it has returned to the past
as all things do

ti trovo bene
vedo che stai bene

i agree   i am well

i bring her Canadian chocolates
caramel sweet
she has no teeth
i am a little ashamed at my
arrogance
my ignorance

this irrelevant little room
where my life   began
was once home

this room where my aunt lies
solitary and   toothless
waiting to go   home

from:

The Invisible Woman

Invisible

i am sitting
once again facing the *Stazione Termini*
once again beneath the cool
of a palm tree
sipping the juice of Sicilian oranges
the cigarette
the book
the brand new city map

the English couple at the next table
deep in conversation   their
matching pierced noses and brows
their purple and blue hair
replacing the afros and bleached red
of my generation

i am back
dowsed in traffic
in fumes   noise and splendour
here again for whatever it is
i am looking for
the invisible woman
no longer young enough to desire
not old enough to need direction

i am middle aged
i walk and sit among crowds
a weightless spirit
my 100 kilos unnoticed
my immense breasts   unimportant

Fellini would have loved me
Fellini should have loved me

now it is only the manicured nail
of time
precisely scratching out
any thought of romance from an
aging heart

i am free   now
to stop in gardens   linger
to read the Latin words
on church walls
to notice how loud birds
can be in the month of March
i am free   now
to walk with the stray mutt
who accompanies me to the gates
of the   *camposanto*
then turns away at the gate
knowing he is not yet ready
for this   *ultima passeggiata*

i recognize my face in the young women
clustered in   *piazzas*
their freshness and anticipation
young bodies aflutter   new butterflies
ready to take in the sweet
to fly   to begin the joyous

i walk to the spaces i have been before
to the fountains and monuments
where i had promised to return
once more
the ritual of coins and wishes

this city is a mosaic of   scattered hearts
multi coloured petals on cobblestones
trampled with time   well worn
into ancient stones
so many pieces brilliant in the sunshine
it is difficult to recognize
the scraps that are   mine

Spanish Steps

i remember flowers in 1976
large pots   lining the stairs
as far up as the church of
Trinità di Monti
maybe i have imagined them
maybe i have wished them

they are not here   now

only bodies and more bodies
young bodies   loitering
women   men   hunters
of tender flesh
peddlers of   romance
but the sun flirts with
everyone regardless of age
or size
it teases equally
and we are in love with the
playground

i know Keats
must have sat here
on these very same steps
his young frail body needing
this Italian sun

he must have scribbled
words and thoughts in a diary
so he would never forget
this place

Piazza Navona

i dine alone
it is a habit
my husband works nights

i dine alone
in *Piazza Navona*
it is a   sin

the waiter is extra attentive
has taken pity on me
a woman   alone   in Rome
a sorrowful sight

a woman of a   certain age
beneath a Roman night sky
in Spring
a half moon dangling over my head
bright as the flirtatious stars

i dine on *amatriciana* and veal
a glass of red wine
my eyes on the gifts of *Bernini*
in the *piazza*
my heart wanting to plunge into
the fountain

i will act out the   game
it is fun to pretend

the waiter's English is less fine
that my Italian   yet
by the end of the meal we are
as close as two   *paesani*

arrivederci
comes with a smile
a touching of hands
two lips on the alluring cheek
of the woman who dines   alone

from:

My Etruscan Face

My Etruscan Face

i am not *Fellini's* dream girl
Gelsomina
with the clownish grin
the sad lost eyes
i am not *Cabiria*
in a fifties celluloid
promenading at midnight
beneath a Roman moon
on an avenue of umbrella pines

that bold goddess Anita
bathing her flawless skin
in Bernini's fountain

my Etruscan face betrays me
faded with time
my profile etched on stone
disintegrates

i am a museum piece
a fresco stumbled upon
by the curious art student
who observes history
in the lines of my face

the grandmother of another century
everything about me sings the past
my skin
my eyes
the fullness of my belly
the art student takes me home
a souvenir

*

we hang beautifully on stone walls
but we don't dance as they did
from the *Arno* down to the *Tiber*
long before the Romans

they are still dancing on the tombs
in *Tarquinia*
the sound of their graceful flutes
inebriated wild boars
then the banquets
life and death

women sat next to their men
entitled

sono ciociara

per Umberto Patriarca

to be alive is to be made of memory
—Philip Roth

i me ne so ita
tant tiemp fa'
er na uagliona
pi*ù* piccula de te
senza storia
e manch ducazion

tu te si state a caseta
nsieme a mammeta
e padrete
nsieme a le sore tije
si ite a la scola
si studiat
te si fatte professor
chiss*à* com'era
cuntenta mammeta
quant t'ha vist sistemat

tu ne si dout part*ì*
si rimast ch'i paesani
ch'i amici tia
pure i
uleua stà a casa mia
ma i ne teneua na casa
e padreme steua tant luntan

i legge le parole che tu si scritt
e me sent tant abbandunata
perch*é* sacce
ca tu si uluto bene
a na terra, a ne paese
si cunusciuto na storia
invence i me la
so douta inventa`
e pure ste dialetto
mezz stuort e sturdit
me fa cap*ì*
la mia cundanna

(*written in the dialect of the region of Lazio, known as Ciociaro*)

i am ciociara

for Umberto Patriarca

to be alive is to be made of memory
—Philip Roth

i went away
a long time ago
i was just a kid
younger than you
without a history
or an education

you stayed home
with your mamma
and your papa
and your sisters
you went to school
studied hard
became a professor
how proud your mother
must have been
when she knew you
were set for life

you didn't have to leave
stayed with the *paisans*
with all your friends
in that little town
me
i wanted to stay home too
but i didn't have a house

and my father was waiting
somewhere far

i read the words you write and
feel abandoned one more time
because i know you loved a land
a town
you had a history
i had to invent mine
and even this half drunk
and broken dialect
i write lets me understand
how condemned i am

Very Very Venice

Coco Bruna lights a cigarette
her lake blue venetian eyes
sparkle beneath her
unnaturally black hair
in a voice ravaged by tobacco
and time
she rumbles out her accented words

dees ees my ceetee
dees ees my
very very Venice
yes?
this *is* her city
her very very Venice
every corner
every laneway
every *piazza* we fall into
each bridge we lumber across
she has known intimately

her fingers slither along
slices of cool ancient marble
feeling the words
the dates
the history
she belongs here like the song of the
gondolieri
she is a Vivaldi symphony
escaping through
lace framed windows

nothing suggests
this might have been
my city
i am forever the stranger
in this peninsula of lost dreams
forever the tourist come
packed with insignificant facts

i know a little something of
Casanova the man the lover
the poet
a little something
of his dramatic escape
by the bridge of sighs
his eternal exile
from the city he loved

i know a little something
of another poet
whose muse
still walks the alleyways at night
a shadow in long skirts

i know a little less about the
intrusion of Turks and Arabs
of imported whores attending
great ships in the harbour

i am not of the sea
i am no mystery
not the elegance of wealth
not of the school of painters
princes
my dialect is the sound
dry rocks make

carried with dust and wind
it is dark skin
assaulted by sun
i cannot sip grappa at sunset
the fire is unpleasant in my throat

*

Coco Bruna is luscious
a woman of beauty and heart
a sister in spirit
a political ally
we are women of the 1970's
revolution and love
warriors with   tongues

Coco Bruna is home
aging well after the battle
accepting the sunset
over her city's sky
sharing it with me
sensing my need

i raise the fine *murano* glass
to my lips
i drink to her *very, very, Venice*
and close my eyes
then i drop another Canadian nickel
into the canal
by the bridge of sighs

The Bottom Drawer

there are only two towels left
two pillow cases
a yellow faded sheet
of heavy linen
one white tablecloth
needing ironing

the bottom drawer
of my mother's dresser
holds all that is left of
my grandmother's hands

there were four sisters
too many brides
to dress
to many grooms to
impress

Angela Maria's hands
never stopped
whether they held a scythe
a pitchfork
a child
or the needle
with the cotton-silk thread

extraordinary hands
strong enough
to clear the fields
and harvest the corn
to shape the cheese
and knead the dough

gentle enough
to ease the pain
elegant enough
to invent a world of roses
on cotton
fields of lilies on
fine linen
trimmed with lace

i hold the pieces in my hands
feel the warmth left there
the force of love
passed on

my mother never uses
these towels any more
the tablecloth
free of stains   folded
placed next to a white
baptismal gown
my grandmother
embroidered for me
the yellow silk threads have
shaped miniature stars

i close the drawer
until the next time
my heart needs a reminder
of what amazing
breathing   tools
we are

Italia

i walk down your streets
and i am a beggar
my hand extended
wanting something from you
that i can hide inside me forever

the *Duomo* in the distance
beautiful and   unreal

my feet at its magnificent doors
i cannot enter   the majesty
i am so insignificantly small

Italia once again
you have robbed me
with eyes wide open
you have taken me
from the beginning to
the cab ride
you have emptied my pockets
and i have barely arrived

Summer in Georgian Bay

i drive north
highway 400 to the Holland Marsh
where the summer green is fading
but glorious fruit and
vegetables in late summer
are bountiful
i park by the side of the road
look over the flatness
in the distance
the red and brown roof of the
farmhouse   clouds napping
there are pieces of this province
i love

the turquoise water of Georgian bay
the silhouette of Blue Mountain
the long drive with the window open
watching the sun rehearse its magic
on open fields of tall corn
giant bales of hay ready
to greet the coming of winter

i walk to the rocky hem of the bay
scooping the clear cool water
bringing it to my face
wanting it desperately to taste
of salt

Poppies Are Red

still that inconsolable girl
under all the façade
still running through poppies
hiding under their skirts

you trample them with your
large feet
in your determined hunt
you don't hear their cry

when you trap me
i lie breathless   i am red
so red
you cannot tell us apart
i am safe   for a while

That Night There Was Snow

that night there was snow
and moonlight
we played in both
for the first time
together

you said you loved me
as only you could love me
your hands on my eyes
upset the ghosts
startled them away
your words pledged
to make well the past
the sins committed
weren't ours

one reckless lovely
moment in time
there was no one but
you and me
one mouth to speak
our lives
watch them become breath

Another November Visiting You

the sun makes it bearable
unusual sun
out of place in November

nothing chills the heart
like this month

time to stop
i have written about you
enough
the conflicts
the reconciliation
enough
confessions
put an end to it
                                        closure
that modern word
without meaning

nothing in life is ever closed
latched or   forgotten

each time i come here
there is something new
to understand
something new to you

today the oak is golden brown
leaves strewn among the headstones
the Japanese maple still
holding on to its red
competing with the yellow

of the poplar
what a carnival
around this bench

i sit and scribble
my words

your picture faces the sun
i cannot see you clearly
but you are there
this is the 23rd year
you would have been
an old man now
close to my age
we might have talked now

you did not garden much
preferring smoky spaces
with loud voices
and a hand full of aces

but i am sure you like this place
i chose for you
the sun in your face   the colours
erase November

Zia Assunta

my *zia Assunta*   the third sister
something about the number three
a little mystical   a little special
but all my aunts   were special

unique in their beauty their intensity
their largeness i have inherited
their love of children i have embraced

zia Assunta
grown old and beautiful still
elegant in her white hair
and blue dress
the tiny gold and coral earrings

i hear her voice
in the *vico*   of my town
her songs
we played in the square
by the *cartiera*
where my uncle *Bernardo*
labored for years to earn their bread
until he got that awful disease
that took his voice
and then his life
that cold little stone house
my cousin *Cristina* scrubbed clean
every inch   till the stones
were smooth as   marble
a palace to her obsession

that town offered little
but was abundant in sunshine
and my cousins and i
happy discovering rocks
and birds and snails

then we crossed an ocean
at different times
met up again in the land
of dreams
                sleep well my aunt
the children are fine

Prodigal Daughter Returns

the multitudes have left
back to the residences
assembled in suburbs
the old church is empty
except for me
and your clay body spread out
on the cotton sheet
half-naked on the altar
the few flickers of candlelight
are electric
not even the smell of wax i remember

there is movement in the basement
statues dragged to their corners
covered up until the next Good Friday

i have waited to cry
now that you are alone
cry for my dead cousin
whose journey ended yesterday
for my father who left long ago
for my friend who wasn't ready
but had to go

i need the silence to speak to you
but you crave the thousands
to celebrate your credibility

i am your lost disciple
the prodigal daughter
a stray
i do not serve you in the

proper way
am i still welcome
do i still please
or am i an embarrassment

the liberties i take
against your servants
are they punishable
the pews i do not polish
the flowers i won't arrange
the fantasies i will not indulge

did you fear death that night
for just one second
that night in the garden
were you afraid

was there too much silence
as your brothers slept
their dreams so far
from your pain

Peeling Onions

> i promised i would never turn you into poetry, but
> allow this liar these willful, wicked lines
> —Gwendolyn MacEwan

your world changes
one Saturday afternoon
between four p.m. and suppertime
while you open a can of tomatoes
peel an onion
sauté the beef medallions
your little girl likes

but she doesn't want supper
with you tonight
it is the first of countless suppers
she will not want with you
she tells you why
and your world transforms
something dies

children kill you quickly
because they can
one look
one word
one secret
they erase you
your tears are all yours now

what is there left to say
go and live what is left of your life
one day when they are peeling an onion
they may recall
a moment *once upon a time*

Escape Land

you disappear
pollen   on butterfly wings
scraps from a tablecloth
shaken free
swallowed by spectator birds

your name is the sound of
an enraged sea   powerful
beautiful

something to run to
and to run from
a dangerous love
my heart   a ravenous
solitary wound

you are my mother's young breast
smeared with sea salt
sprinkled with spices
to distract my lips
convince them you are empty
no more sweet
temperate milk of life

the red lips of a new romance
i taste you still
you fill my mouth   a first love
an original sin

you are the counterfeit passion
i cannot do without

one more time you return
before it is too dark
and there is nothing to find
there is nothing you did not take
with you
the rest is a shadow
a prologue to the inevitable
waiting space
                    a landscape
                                        your escape
land

They Call Me Teacher, Teacher

"teacher, teacher
Marco kicked me in the
balls!"
his pudgy fingers over his
private parts

"no, no Jason"
i reacted with concern

"the proper word is
genitals"
the following recess
Jason stormed into class
his hands cupped again
over the delicate spot
his heated eyes and nostrils
fuming

"teacher, teacher
if he doesn't quit it
he's gonna break my
janitors!"

A Sausage for Christmas

when Woolworth's department store
still existed on the corner of
St. Clair and Dufferin Avenue
in the late nineteen seventies
my students spent a lot of time shopping
and shop lifting

when Christmas rolled around
i received the best that
Woolworth's had on sale

a gallon of rose oil body scent
or Evening in Paris perfume
that wouldn't fade
at any measure of scrubbing
clay figurines of assorted cats and dogs
the occasional box of Turtles chocolates
and dozens of coffee mugs that read
the best teacher
but years later
when Joao brought me a large sausage
wrapped in silver paper
i was delighted
"thank-you Joao, it looks delicious"
i gushed

"my mother made it miss, for you
we killed the pig and then
we made a lot of them and this one
is for you"
i assumed   as we sometimes do

"your parents must have a farm
where is your farm Joao?"
"it's on Dovercourt miss
just behind the Starbucks"

Immacolata

how quickly we forget
to remember   the trespasses
and i had promised never to
make the same mistakes with
my own students
we are human   we fail

Immacolata came into my
class at age nine
she was all her name implied
immaculate
                    beautiful
                                    smart

because we shared a mother country
i made an assumption
"*Immacolata,*
that is a beautiful name
but would you rather i called you
by a shorter name   like Maggie?"
her sinuous black eyes gazed
at me without reservation

"my name is *Immacolata,* call me
Immacolata"
but i should have known that

My Common Shirt

it had mother of pearl buttons
i left the top two   undone
the sleeves were long
it covered my backside
the print was subtle
i wore it with   elegance
and a touch of vanity
until Jeffrey   decided
to comment on my   style

"miss, you gots the same shirt like
my mother gots"
"has Jeffrey,   like my mother has"
"yeah miss
she gots the same one
sactly like yours"
"well Jeffrey
 i guess your mother and i shop
at the same store"
"yeah Miss,
                the fat lady store"

Miscellaneous Lives

> you can sing about life or you can try to understand it.
> you can't do both.
> —Irving Layton

it has taken years
lots of them
to bend the fingers out of shape
to point the eyes toward the feet
your body a question mark
but the years are just one moment
and without memory
there is no moment

i can feed you soup from a nice bowl
homemade chicken soup
and you won't know
i've made it fresh
bought the chicken in Kensington
from the Greek
stopped for a glass of blood orange juice
thought of Sicily
do you remember Sicily?

*

they are playing Cuban music
in the Azores Café
the market is cheerful
the sun shines
it is warm
people will spend money today
but these are not people with lots

to spend
the young ones looking for bargains
leftover trends
the rest are lives in between
families to feed
children's plastic boots
you used to shop here

*

the black lady with the bible
stopped me again
and wanted to introduce me to Jesus
i told her she had introduced me
last week   twice
had he forgotten me already
i spoke to her for a while
to be polite
offered her something to eat
but she wasn't hungry

*

dogs have replaced the children
some of them are the size of mules
i remember mules in the market
clopping away in the early morning
tied to carts filled with vegetables
leaving great big pancakes of warm shit
behind them
but that was some other market
you would buy the salty goat cheeses
and the olives
now you tell me they give you
heartburn

*

stopped in at the Portuguese bakery
for some sticky buns
the old men
their tired eyes
the smell of sweat
stale cigarettes
changed my mind
walked to the park
such a sad little park
at the end of winter
that brick toilet
right in the center
used in desperation
garbage resurfaced from last fall
a few pigeons on the shoulder of
the King of Kensington
as he converses with his friend
on the wooden bench
the one who always sits there
who's fallen sweetly into madness

dissolved in a sea of lucidity
a mind set free   out of itself
beyond itself
shedding all the wreckage
rising stronger
in a brighter space
where you are

We Are Still the Wops

in nineteen sixty three
my friend
Raffaele Scianimanico
changed his name
he became   Ralph

his last name became some
Irish/Jewish mix   Shaniman

Ralph Shaniman
the   shani   man
was tired of being a
wop
tired of being called
wop
tired of looking
wop
tired of all
that word
implied
greaser
gambler
garlic smelling
spaghetti eating
gangster *Guido*
goomba

in 1964 Ralph
vanished
took a dive
out of my life
went off
to lose himself

far from the village
the wops
called home
away from
the garlic
the alleged
gangsters
away from the
bricklayers

away from the
dressmakers
homemakers
winemakers
away from the
factory mamas
and working papas
from the
hairdressers
hotel maids
pool halls and
garden spades

arrivederci sister
good bye brother
Ralph went somewhere
to find a brand new face

the rest of us
stayed
with our names
long
and unpronounceable

funny
fantastic
and farcical

we poured a little sugar
on the bitter
learned to duck the blows
swallowed slowly
didn't choke

fifty years to build a city
sweat
blood and imagination

a little love
a little passion
daily bread
and daily prayer
a penny earned
another saved
a baby here
another there
and here
                    we are
Ralphie

but when one or two of us
is found with throats slit open
drenched in blood
no facts   no proof
nothing but a long
unpronounceable name
nothing else
to assure their claim

we are the gangster wops again

seems the hitmen
          always get their
goomba

Cappuccino to Go

the morning barman
has made twenty-three coffees
since i sat down and ordered mine
i watch and count
he steams the milk till the foam
spills over the side of the stainless
steel pot
then steadily pours the exact amount
checking the colour
making sure it blends into a caramel
brown and then dusts shavings
of bitter cocoa on top

sixteen were to go
the rest are scattered about
the early risers
their heads in assorted papers
wasted eyes hoping to awaken
before they get to where
they will spend their day
he will spend his here
behind the shabby bar
stained mirror behind him
assorted photographs of babies
scotch taped to the wall next
to a faded dollar bill

it doesn't matter what the weather
is outside
he unlocks the door at seven and by
eight o'clock the espresso machine
sings arias

the aroma from its chromed lungs
gliding out the crack above the door
the tall beer mug
clinks
with coins of appreciation
each time another cup goes out

when the mug is full
his day is almost done

The Gatto Nero

the corner of Crawford street
and College
has made room for an old friend
not out of sentiment
nothing on College Street
is about sentiment anymore
it is lifestyle
it is youth
it is money

the old *Gatto*
began as a kitty in the 1960's
smoky and somber
my father and his
dispossessed buddies
drank Carmine's espresso
in little cups
played cards
late into the night
men intimate with
whatever bonds them

women stayed away
never entered the consecrated doors
i ventured in on occasion
as a child
to remind my father
he had another home
where my mother waited
as supper got cold

the *Gatto* was a haven
for men in exile
safe from anything Canadian
safe from the anger and
disappointment of wives

When Women Talk

the world cracks open
like a watermelon
you never know whether
it will be ripe and sweet
or a dry stringy   squash

she says she stays because
he loves her
her need to be loved
is much stronger than
her need to love

a wound somewhere long ago
she needs the comfort
the safety

but she wonders about
passion
what desire is like
lust for a body the abandon
the power   the sex

she says she is comfortable
in his arms
sees in his eyes what
he searches for in hers
makes herself believe
it is enough
                                        plenty
a lot more than some
how greedy can one be
he does not stray far

an anchor
all so comforting
but familiar
            so familiar

A Whore in the Confessional

he asked where i put my hands
when i went to sleep at night
i couldn't answer
because i didn't know

that was forty three years ago

perhaps it was curiosity
or
that pain in the ass guilt
rambling around
making you crazy
that led me to the church
one Saturday afternoon

i remember following
the old widows
the old men
and the choir ladies slowly
a few steps behind

confessions
between four and five

God's house is different
on Saturday i thought
calm
few lights or candles burning
just a handful of souls
up and down the long space
silent saints slightly dusty

the priest arrived
without the usual fanfare
sat behind the velvet curtain

one by one
the women and old men
lined up to enter
the little space where
sins are deposited and the
resurrection begins

most were quick   a minute or two
an hail Mary an Our Father
job done
i waited at the end of the line
a little nervous
trying to remember
forty three years of transgressions

someone was abusing
their contracted time
i heard two women cackle
under their breath
  "only a whore
could have so much
to confess"
the back door is open
i turn towards it
my hands are in my pockets

The Dressmaker

for Maria

she has been shaping material
around my body for decades
cottons and silks
wool knits and polyesters
that refuse ironing
my preferred Italian linens
light, cool
she has chalked and pinned
my mutable shape like a map
standing on a stool
to reach my shoulders

this sixty inch woman
with thinning hair and dusky eyes
this woman from the stony heels
of the *Maiella*
a town where the almonds
taste sweet
stained with sunlight and a
coating of honey

this ordinary woman
has landed in the basement
of a suburban house
in a country of maple and snow

a singer sewing machine
a table and mismatched chairs
tape measure, scissors
necessary small things

it is 1973 and she will still be here
in the year 2000
among her spools and threads
boxes of used patterns
a devoted cassette player

serenades her long nights
only the music has assisted her
triumphs, her mistakes

the skin of her fingers shines
it is thin, buffed
polished like wood
but the digits of her hands
are liquid
they are a violin
the sly footwork of a tango
precise
each stitch
each blouse is
a rose tattoo

the dressmaker
serves espresso along with the
fantasy
and the women return again and
again
for the gowns that create the
illusion
for the skirts that hide the
indulgences
they return for the white dress
with the brilliant pearls
each sewn individually
such pride

in another place
another time
her hands might have carved
angels in stone

here she patches wings
to help them fly

Lupins and Tangerines

for Dorothy

Let me tell you a secret: there is
no such thing as an uninteresting life.
—Rohinton Mistry

i will not eat a tangerine
without thinking of you
your old straw hat
filled with them
on the wicker chair
by your kitchen door
the purple lupins in the garden
the white roses growing tall

you were not a gardener
you admitted
not like Ena or Rob
but you were happy there
in your modest bungalow
on Middle Road
not far from town
a quick dash to the shops
in your mini orange car

that lovely night
in January
gin tonics and sherry
and talk
talk
talk

while the moon
slipped out of the belly
of that enormous sleeping giant
expanding
high above the Havelock hills

you found me exotic
this tall dark girl
in your nephew's hand

mysterious
the way Naples and Capri
must have been in 1943
when you sailed away
on that Red Cross Ship

i don't know if you ever
touched the soil of my
peninsula
perhaps only your eyes
were occupied with the blue
and the pain
of that tortured land
but decades later
i came to tell you all about it

you listened
as if i had brought you
diamonds
but you understood words
were priceless

that evening with Bernard
and his gentleman's adventures
the romantic interludes

of both our hearts
ageless

when you are home
in that other garden
where the apple trees are
strong
there will be gardeners
among the roses and
purple lupins
waiting
with sherry sweet
and lots of tangerines

Kapiti

for Bernard Lur

Bernard painted it beautifully
in the light of the afternoon
in mid-January
the ocean holding it in its
clear blue palm

i have the painting in my
Grace Street living room
a gift from the artist
who kissed my hand that
summer evening in Dorothy's
garden
while we sipped dry sherry
the romance of English gentlemen
in their eighties

at twenty-nine i was living the movie
i was Rita Hayworth
loving the scent of tangerines
in the wicker bowl
loving the artist
the cricket-player
in his white elegance

Kapiti hangs in my living room
all the way from the bottom
of the world
that long white cloud
in the Pacific

i lose myself in it
missing Bernard
missing the ocean
at Paraparaumu
where you and i dug for *pipis*

our naked feet
deep in the sand
we watched the Maori children
fishing off the rocks
the long walks at
that enchanted hour
just before the sea gulps down
that last piece of sun

then off to the chip shop
at Bottle Creek
hoping to get a glimpse
of Sam Hunt by the water
singing his poems

we bought *paua* fritters
and a dozen oysters
drank that half gallon of white wine
waiting for the moon to erupt

tell me again
where is paradise

I Should Have Walked into Your Garden

for Gwendolyn MacEwan

you died the year
i gave birth to my only child
twenty years later
you are born again in my heart

i had read your words before
without concentrating
always in the rush of life
i know now
we could have been good friends

i should have walked into your garden
that afternoon on Brunswick Avenue
when i saw you through
Priscilla's kitchen window
while we poured wine for
somebody's birthday
you sat in the rattan chair
in your long skirt
your black hair tied back

it was a cup you sipped from
sitting there among the
green leaves of a Toronto August
i imagined iced tea cooling your throat
you looked up
your captivating eyes

i should have walked into your garden
that Saturday afternoon
when i was young
but you were too perfect
to disturb that afternoon
alone in your world
fighting the dark angels
conjuring up words to leave behind

i watched you for a while
sipped my wine
i was not yet ready
to be your friend

How Temporary We Are

more than
just a sad woman
she is a woman
with doubts

an unoccupied space
among
the collected clutter
of her life
among
the boxes labeled
with permanent marker

the largest box
marked
things of the heart
the smallest
has no label at all
miscellaneous
unnecessary things
that cannot be parted with

the dust is established
in the corners of the room
the floor has been swept
but not really
windows
will be washed
in time
and cheap cleansers
will remove any trace
of who she was

bookshelves
holding new things
will not question
what was there before

she will leave a plant
or two behind
hoping they will survive
root themselves
in new pots
but the plants will die
replaced

we are one breath
the measure of time
from beginning to end
and all is erased

the soul is clean
again
pure
white
without fault
without sin
or experience
only the question remains
the unavoidable question
unaltered

it allows her to lose herself
in ordinary things
in the mundane acts
she repeats for assurance

she will delight
in her child's voice
find comfort in the strong hands
of a tall husband
the good night tumbling down
from the third floor of her house

she will raise a glass with her friends
she will drink the wine

as bright as the sun is today
the cloud
will surely come

the tree will quiver with wind
the glorious blossom will fall
murmuring
                    murmuring
how temporary we are

Il Giglio

for Elizabetta

they are tall
elegant
ladies at a garden party
standing in their finest
warbling on about nothing
sipping the afternoon away
without concern

they are a blue-purple velvet
the colour of royal drapes
inside the private towers
of privileged eyes

in her garden they were white
and grew by the gate where
Elizabetta fell on the rocks
that inconceivable day
a bloodless crevice on
the back of her head
she had just learned to walk

her mother wailed
by that gate for years
on her knees
on the same stones
that had absorbed her blood
until that lamb appeared
by moonlight one night

her mother stopped wailing
after that
went on weeping in private
i remember the white iris
their lambs ears
floppy and soft in the
midnight light
in summer
they grew there
every year
among the rocks by the gate

Secrets

how can i tell you my secrets
you are sure i have none
i am a woman without secrets
you think
i am your mother
transparent woman
housekeeper without clandestine
undergrounds
i have never been your age
never had my heart in an earthquake

you are the curator of all the keys
i wait for you to forget to lock a door
some night
when you are racing
towards the uncertainty of your life

i am your cliché
well dog-eared

you have a craving
for new and improved
metaphors
i hope you find them
my love

Ontario

i knew a boy once who loved pigeons
hunted garter snakes in the ravine
at the end of our street
jumped over fences
by the railroad tracks
skipped the
wooden planks two by two
daring the trains
until he reached Gerrard Street
Lucky's Smoke and Gift
where he filled his pockets
with gum and licorice sticks
he tried hard
to teach me how to hide them
but i always got caught

i knew a boy once
who loved horses
and motorcycles
learned to ride one in his teens
joined a club with other boys
in love with speed
vagabonds
he had two brothers
my uncle's Canadian sons

my uncle who married the pretty
Sicilian girl
brought her to a dead end
Toronto street
by the railroad track

half Sicilian they were
my boy cousins
a bond much tighter
than my Roman clan

half Sicilian east end boys
something i could never
be part of
something i could never
understand

i knew a boy once
who spoke a language
he had figured out for himself
some
Canadian-Sicilian-Roman mantra
bizarre sounds
squeezed out through a colander
an attempt to communicate

my uncle dismissed the effort
it didn't sound right
my aunt was too numb from
the noise of trains

i moved away to the west end
the boys stayed
we got older   lost touch
lived our lives
i heard he'd had a rough time
toughed it out

i met his children
only once
among the flowers

the handshakes
i recognized their half Sicilian eyes
beautifully dark

my uncle's first born son was named
Ontario

from:
Too Much Love

Too Much Love

And each day the gap narrows
and each day the fury grows
—Antonia Pozzi

time to improvise the happiness
arrange an alibi
time to go before the mirror
an anarchist

once again a relocation
postmarked by the last third
of this life

the time that counts
the difference-maker
the weight-loser
the turn-it-all-around period
without blood

the poems are written
the child is grown

you are tangential
but you are loved
hold on

My Name is Giovanna Berta

i get my names
from my two uncles
Giovanni and *Umberto*
one a soldier   the other
a *bonvivant*
one died of the clap
the other a bullet

grandpa was a communist
with a dent in his skull
from the great war
his oldest son wore
a black shirt in *Mussolini's* clan
marched tall and proud
in those leather boots

my father was the youngest
a prisoner of war in Sardinia
with the Americans   who had food
he learned to cook their meals
on that rocky sheep-infested island
for more than a year

mamma was sixteen
when the Germans sent her
out   pail in hand
to fetch water from a well
while the air raids bombed
the countryside

the shrapnel has left scars

mamma met a soldier
from Sicily   married him in 46
he died in 48
my father loved her
                                        later

i was born when it was quiet
before the evacuation
the *terranuova*

i listen to her stories
continue battling
the contradictions
in my blood

Translating the Sea

i am so far from the sea
i dream of it constantly

mamma tells me
water is
a bad sign
so are teeth
don't dream of water or
teeth
or
flying

mamma spends hours
on the phone with
her sisters
their lives
their pain
their bank accounts

then they decode
the dreams

i lie
when she asks about mine
terrified
she will discover
how often i fly
over the ocean
dropping big white teeth
into the waves

Silenzio

you spare me the truth
you think i rest better

what i don't know about you
is worse than
any truth

what i conjure in my head
can stop my heart

i count the mistakes
regrets
the words we
never spoke
when we should have

the absolute waste
of love   disguised

the regrettable silence

At This Age

at this age
i love things
differently

without the need
to jump into the well
the deepest part of
the lake

i am drawn to the calm
the grace
of an ordinary day
my mother's hands

at this age
i applaud what is
foolish   absurd
i'm a spectator

how sweet now
the resistance to argue

Birthday Poem Wish

my husband tries hard
to erase my sadness
and i become
more sad
because i cannot be happy
for him

Love Disguised

after the romance
there is tolerance
or violence
the journalist
writes

so many uncertainties
half truths
between spoken lines
written lines
the headline
a suburban bungalow
in the month of March
a woman silenced
by knives

too much space
between Brampton
and Mumbai
not enough gold
to sanctify a marriage

veils too thin
to conceal deception

everywhere
stunning fabrics
disguised as love

Allow Me

i read somewhere
that poetry written
by women
is always
sub-standard
weak
unstructured
merely
sentimental
domestic at best

allow me the fantasy
the myth
that i can be part of
the chorus

i can step on the stage
and we can split the
applause

Mamma at 87

> my mother's face returns
> to the fireside
> —Rocco Scotellaro

you've told me that story before
but i let you enjoy it again

you cry at the parts
you remember best
the easier times
so you say
even the war
under the airplanes
the hunger
that handsome soldier
with the mustache
your first love
Sicily
the widow you were
at twenty-two
that ship across the Atlantic
endless

sometimes you even remember
my father

you go on
another coffee
another fruit
a cracked walnut

your memories
my inheritance

*

after the talk
i move towards the door
i go and write
try to cheat death
with my words
gamble with time

but the cuffs are tight
on my wrists
like the sleeves of that
undersized uniform
the nuns made me wear
when you left me in their
company
all those years
when papa was away

you had to work
i needed someplace safe
you thought
but the nuns were just
a place

who will know me
this much
this way

i will write the stories
for you
one day

Reading the Women Who Loved

Sylvia Plath was
Lady Lazarus
baited by death

"Dying
is an art,"
she wrote

"like everything else,
I do it exceptionally well."
if life had been
a kinder lover
there would have been
more poems

*

you wonder why
we bother to love at all

time invested
touching
tears
lunacy in the end
wasted time

*

if i were honest
i would spell it out

poetry is a screen
for cowards

nightmares don't lie
they revisit with
the same vengeance
night after night
climb in your bed
stalking your sleep

you've hidden another body
killed someone else
your eyes open
you remove the blankets
look under the bed
convince yourself
it isn't there

what resilient creatures
we are
to endure it all
keep going

Clever Girl

they will reject you
clever girl you are
more than i imagined

you see things
in the daylight
i pretend
i live in the night

you are sure
my heart is blocked

an old fraud

you have seen through
its perforations
where it was gnawed

you confront the
impostor
sluggish muscle
without purpose

they will refuse you

this broken down
beating weight
tells me
they will be alarmed
by your truth

the god they
made me swallow
in thin
round
salt free
mouthfuls
will snub you

no status for your kind
among the chosen

the incense
the hymns
the communion
of things done right
you are all wrong

there is no place for me
either
at their table

i choose hell
before i deny you

*

you are stronger
than i will ever be
i claim some responsibility
for that
not the blood that runs
through our veins
type 0 positive

but all those nights
in my arms
in my bed
all the stories
poems

endless hours
with the oxygen mask
after the attacks
the tiny pills
that made your
heart race

you laughed through it all
held my hand
kept it steady

i am happy you are strong

The Boy Loves You

poured his heart out
after the third beer
the bottle of white wine
two *campari* and soda

the boy loves you
poor half-starved
unfortunate soul

said i had done
a good job
shouldn't blame myself

the boy wants to love you
forever
wants you to love him
forever

what can i do
i feed him
i listen
i mix the *campari* and soda

he's all wrong
but the boy loves you

Accept Me

you need to construct
a demon to rebel against

i am perfect
he is perfect
we are your
perfect monster
i understand

i fought my own
long before you were
a consideration

you find it all
so comical

Just Be

> Each to his grief, each to
> his loneliness and fidgety revenge
> —Gwendolyn Brooks

who am i to judge your love
who am i to know what your
heart swells with
what your body needs
what it feels warm against
comfortable with

what eases your day
making it blithe
giving it meaning

who am i to understand
what broken thing inside
becomes whole
when she is there

i only want your thoughts
to fit my schedule
your laughter to come into
my room
when i need it most

whatever sin
they have branded
you with
i will forgive
come home

when you want
i will not lock the door
nothing to fear
my heart is
what it has always been
a place you will find
refuge

A New Dare

i burden you with
my dreams

they weigh on you
because they are not
your dreams   but mine
always mine
even when i envision them
for you

when you were safe
in story books and rhyme
i dreamed them for you

when all you wanted
was warmth
and cookies from a jar

now they are not
part of your plan
your agenda is full
with other cravings

i apologize
you apologize
but nothing untangles
the nature
of who we are

*

make me understand
this place you go to
that terrorizes
erases all i had designed
for us

these pitiable imaginings
i thought were
the right ones
nothing but splinters
under the skin

make me feel
what your smile
seems to know
the uncomplicated reason
for falling in love
believing it is all that matters
all that is reasonable
and real

you taunt me
with a new dare
now that the games
are done
a new defiance
too precarious to occupy

how do i master the
latest technology

seems only my pen
outlines my heart

Another Road

on a painting by Patsy Berton

most alluring
when it is silent

compacted and washed
by rain and time

a long continuous curve
slips through trees

infinite
unlimited

carving history without
sound or blade

The Clothesline

on a painting by Patsy Berton

Mrs. *Rondinelli* did laundry
every Monday and Friday
rain or shine
whatever the season

i was greeted by her
husband's socks
marching eastward
long and woolen
all in a row
pinned one by one with
wooden pegs
all facing the same direction
the blue checkered shirts followed
arms extended and free
in breezy conversation
with the early morning air
then came the pants
the polka-dotted boxers
endless procession of male apparel

the feminine under-things
reserved for a second line
girdles and sensible cottons
the flannel nightgowns
buttoned up
towels
white gleaming sheets
proudly in the middle

at the very end were the teenage panties
lace bras that belonged to her youngest

Mrs. *Rondinelli* would stand
for long quiet moments
arms folded under her weighty breasts
her serious eyes fixed
on the orderly clothesline
radiant in the morning light
her crisp, controlled world
clean   without intrusion

Tony's Car

on a painting by Patsy Berton

in the laneway
behind Crawford Street
between the maple and the magnolia
he'd back it up   gradually
making sure not to decapitate
the hollyhocks and geraniums
his mother had planted

stopping where the cement
bordered the grass
he'd park his new baby
turn off her lights
and lounge there a while

then he'd open the door
step out in slow motion
observe the shiny silver chrome
slide his warm hand the length
of her polished cobalt blue shell
kiss his fingers
and leave her to the night

Hagar

on a painting by M.C. Conlon

it is always the women
angels
servants
whores
and wives

bearing sons
always sons

to inhabit the glory
the throne

occupy the sacred
passing of time

A Girl Made of Lavender

i can still smell Lynne's white starched blouse
her see-through white skin glowing
as i sat in the seat next to her
at Gledhill Public School

Lynne was the first Canadian girl
i saw when i walked into Mrs. Riley's
third grade class

Lynne looked like Canada
Lynne smelled like Canada

my black uncombed curls
and homemade dress
made me feel ashamed
i was unscented
and without starch

from that first day
when i sat beside her
i wanted to be Lynne
i wanted to smell like Lynne

i learned later
her perfect starched clean blouse
was sprayed with lavender

Lynne was forever stuck
inside my nose
a girl made of lavender

Darrel and Billy were both
in love with Lynne
and she knew they were
every time she took the Jersey milk
chocolate bars they stole for her
from Henry's five and ten cent store

it was always a contest
who could earn her love
with the sweetest candies
the best chocolate
stolen from the candy store
just for her

Billy got caught once
Henry dragged him to the principal's office
Billy's mother had to come to school
she was really mad
she screamed and yelled so loud
we could hear her down the hall

but it didn't stop Billy
he just switched stores

the next day he brought Lynne caramels
he'd picked up at Woolworth's at the corner of
Danforth and Woodbine

Darrel followed Lynne everywhere
every recess and every lunch hour
after school he'd wait by the fence
till she appeared
his eyes crammed with her white beauty
her clean ironed clothes
and her sweet smell

Sometimes Darrel brought Lynne
little glass statues of animals
wrapped in pink Kleenex
he kept them in his pocket
until Lynne appeared
then he would hand them to her
with a smile that showed all
his teeth

i wondered where he got them from
they looked expensive
but he never told anyone

every week like magic
a new animal made of glass
wrapped in pink Kleenex
came out of his pocket

Darrel loved animals
he loved horses
and drew them on big sheets
of coloured paper
they looked almost real
like pictures taken with a camera

he drew the horses for Lynne
but she preferred the little glass animals
she always threw the drawings away

Darrel and Billy lived for Lynne
other boys made fun of them
but Darrel and Billy didn't care
they guarded Lynne like a princess
protected her from anything
that didn't shine like she did

made sure she always had
plenty of sweet caramels
and glassy things to keep her company

Lynne hardly ever played with girls
she never once played with me

Lynne had tiny perfect ears
like beautiful shells from the sea
i could see them because her hair was
always in a ponytail
tied with a blue ribbon

the elastic that held my curls together
was thick and brown

Lynne's head was just the right size
i would stare at it sometimes
watch her ponytail swish back and forth
hoping that once, just once
she would turn and see me
she never did

Mrs. Riley wasn't sure
what to do with me
the day i walked into her class
she sat me next to Lynne
hoping her light would somehow
creep into me
it never did

i tried to copy everything Lynne would do
the way she sat up straight at her desk
the way she held her head up
on her skinny long neck

staring at the blackboard
even when there was nothing
on the blackboard to look at

i watched how her fingers
moved her pencil
how she printed her letters
her numbers so neatly
between the lines on the workbook page

i tried to do the same
but i never understood why
the numbers and letters
had to stay so neatly between the lines

Lynne never told me why
neither did Mrs. Riley

The day Cristina came into our room
Mrs. Riley moved me
to the back of the class
next to Brenda
who didn't have a smell at all
but was very tall

Cristina was new to Gledhill Public
she came from an island
in the middle of the ocean
a place called Greece

Mrs. Riley didn't know what to do with her
either
but she must have thought
Cristina needed Lynne more than i did

because she gave her my seat

i didn't want to move
i liked sitting next to Lynne
even if she never looked at me
or talked to me
sitting next to Lynne made me feel
that i belonged   a little
sitting next to Lynne made me think
that one day
i could smell like   lavender
that someday
someone would steal Jersey milk chocolate bars
just for me

i wanted to sit next to Lynne forever
but now Cristina
needed Lynne more than i did
Cristina's sad crossed eyes
told me that

i moved next to Brenda
who had no smell at all

Brenda's tall head hid Lynne's pretty ears
Brenda's hair didn't move
it just sat flat and brown
without ribbons
she chewed her fingernails
one by one
spitting the bits on the pages of
Run Spot, Run

*

It was a long walk down Danforth Avenue
to Woodbine from Gledhill Public
nobody lived as far from the school as i did
except Cristina

she lived on Aldergrove Avenue
the dead end street near the railway track
i lived on Moberly
the street that led to the railway track

Lynne lived a few houses from the school
she went home for lunch every day
her mother always waited on the veranda

Cristina and me ate our big messy sandwiches
in the school yard

Sometimes Cristina followed me home
two or three steps behind me
if i stopped she stopped
if i moved she moved
one day i just turned around
talked to her
she didn't understand me much
and i didn't understand her
but we walked together anyway

she had these funny crossed eyes
that stared at her own nose
i wanted to laugh a little
but i never did.
The day Mrs. Riley left
to have her baby Lynne cried
that day Lynne looked different
when i watched tears slide down

her perfect face
leaving little wet spots
on her clean blouse
i felt really sad

i was sure that girls made of lavender
with seashell ears and ponytails
who ate jersey milk chocolate bars
would never have to cry.
The new teacher wasn't nice like Mrs. Riley
the new teacher was full of freckles
her lips cracked at the side and
spit gathered in the tiny cracks
when she talked

the new teacher sat Cristina next to me
the last seat by the window
in the fifth row
i couldn't see Lynne anymore
from where i was sitting
i couldn't smell her
or watch her ponytail bounce
back and forth
her perfect head and sea shell ears
disappeared.
Cristina's ears were big and round and
she wore a small gold loop in each one
Cristina didn't chew her fingernails
she didn't smell like lavender
she didn't look like Canada
and her hair was sort of wild

we sat together in the last two seats
of the fifth row
where nobody ever passed by

but from that day on
we walked home together
after school every day

we saved our coppers for a while
when we had saved enough
we went to Woolworth's
and bought a miniature bottle of lavender
sprayed it all over our clothes
all over our hair and skin
but we didn't smell like Lynne at all

it wasn't long before we realized
lavender
would never smell the same on
girls like us.

Risorgimento

the boys are at it again
my south
is bigger than yours

behind the castles
or the barns   orgasms
of hand and tongue
a blade   and then
the butchery

women wait
it will be the season of rape
soon enough

the south will rise again.
the sadness we inherited
from ancestors
all the reasons that moved us
                    around the world
the massacre
the abandonment
the kick in the ass

it should have made us
stronger smarter kinder

it should have brought us
closer
we should have   talked

but the bitter lingers
on self-serving lips
the taste of venom
still so thick   so sweet

The Fall of Rome

gluttons have eaten this city
for lunch

left crumbs for pigeons
and tourists who
gather in the *piazza*

the charm has faded
along with the glory
there is greed now
and   indifference

Fellini is dead
Pasolini is dead
so is *Magnani*
                                        and the myth
no blonde goddess beckoning
for *Marcello*
and there are fewer coins
in the fountain

terror wears a suit and tie
difficult to detect
children are learning the trade

art is an   amulet
a counterfeit copy
the euro enters the
                                      Vatican
no passport needed

Prince Edward County

for my husband

hollyhocks stand
at attention
under a mackerel sky

Wapoos Island
a giant lily pad
drifting
on lake Ontario

Bruce Cockburn
hitches a ride
along highway 81
while we head east
to visit the loyalists

we'll pour the new
county wines
toast another summer
another moon
another flight
maybe get a little drunk

Pier 21/Halifax, Nova Scotia

it is my anniversary

after fifty years
i visit a port
where a ship once docked

a cemetery
of names on bricks

photographs of faces
in distress
toy ships with detail
cardboard suitcases
hold nothing
frayed wool caps
positioned on hooks

some of us have come
to walk to the gravesite
read ourselves
into the past
hoping to understand
something profound
recognize something
special

all i can recall is water
and a belly upside down

here is where i landed
fifty summers ago
but this is another place
now

When You're 64

for Philip Conlon

Philip our first home
has forgotten us

we raced out the back door
with all those ideals
inside our pockets
the little red book
of some foreign hope
Dylan on the radio and the
revolution

was it the seventies
or earlier than that
it's all a little blurry now

your American accent
Brooklyn or the Bronx
that giant poster of Verdi
on your kitchen wall
Gramsci and Marx
on the table

did we really want
to change the world
from Dufferin and St. Clair
we ate *gelato*
while Bobby Sands starved

remember Nicaragua and Chile
Victor Jara   the massacre
Violeta's ode to life
and Viet Nam

was it all so long ago
when change was promising
and now
from the Empire State
Manhattan
has a sad new   skyline

The Garden on Kaka Street

for Ena and Gia

there's a photo of nana
and you
under the pear tree
in the Kaka Street garden
you are three
nana is old

you climb the low branches
determined
she holds her arm out
to protect you

the pears you pull
will be sliced
eaten with cheese
at suppertime
after the ham and the
kumara

you will want them with
ice cream
vanilla

you don't climb trees
anymore
you haven't climbed them
in years

you don't eat fruit much
either
especially not pears
but i slice them still
hide them in ice cream

while some other child
learns to climb
fruit trees

Otaki Hills

for Robin and Stuart

so much of who i am
is made up of hills

their morning whisper
their midday sleep

their blue lullaby
under that long white cloud

Poets of Water and Wilderness

for Atwood and Musgrave

Margaret and Susan have come
to *Procida* on paper

Canadian mermaids
ocean goddesses
rising from the seas
and dark lakes

enchanting creatures
who mesmerize
take the reader to a land
of mystery and space

they distract *paesani*
from their own sea fish gods
who have been caught
for centuries
in the seaweed of indifference
left quietly to drown
in unfamiliar waters

Procida, the Island

for Oriana

we are sleeping in Sofia's bed
the young concierge tells us
it is the room she requests
each time she comes to the island
just a short boat ride from *Pozzuoli*
where she was born

the balcony looks down on the marina
where Troisi met Neruda
and traded metaphors
for his final performance

men were exiled here
walls too tall to escape from
sea everywhere
lemons large as suns

something in this beauty
the calm
blue mystery
and passing time
makes you hopeful

The Turnabout

the landscape i used to dream about
does not hug me anymore
like my grown daughter
it does not feel the need

i resist falling into sentiment
cannot stay long anyway
always less than the time before

this place is almost done
the rhythm here is bad
for my heart

L'Altra Italia Lives Here

dropped in
by invitation only

another *Villa* in Woodbridge
marble pillars at the gate
vespas on the cobbled drive
fountains without coins

Michelangelo's David
glittering in mosaic
at the bottom of the pool

chefs catering
prosecco bubbling
and wine, wine,
wine

beautiful wives strewn about
Brazilian waxed
and bronzed

the men light the cigars

Ah life in Canada!
dolce
the other *Italia* lives well
doing just fine

cin cin!

The Gambler's Daughter

for Father Gianni

the gambler You are
reminds me of my father
he never had much luck
had no time for You at all
left the prayers to mamma
and me

i have learned them all
backwards and forwards
mamma can even sing them
in Latin
and she does   incessantly

her beads have changed more
than colour in a lifetime
she believes in You still
without argument
something about love
and family keep her strong

i am the one You torment
keep testing

which card to play this time around
love, death, pain
the big "C"
here comes another loss
there goes another flower
appropriated for Your estate

i am left to re-pot the space
re-organize

i never liked to gamble
found it sad
desperate
like papa's eyes when he lost

but You dwell in it
defeat makes you stronger
how is that?
tonight i will pick up the beads
the red crystal ones
join mamma on the couch
hoping   i'll get lucky
stay tough

from:

Donne Italiane ed Altre Tragedie (Italian translation)

'Sta vita

(dialetto Cepranese)

chi se le fusse mai credut
'sta vita
quanta pass che sso fatt
quanta giorn se n'au ite
quanta piante e sacrificie
e alla fine
che te lass
figlia mia
che te lass …
na casa   piccula
ma pagata
chella medaglia d'oro
che padrete me dett
me l'au rubata
nient solde e nient oro
figlia mia
                    ma
quant cose i te dess
ma sule ste` dialett ma rimast
ste dialett che quase quase
n'capisce
è ne regale senza prezz
è na specie di poesia
e quand stiame insieme
zitte zitte
calme calme
sient …… sient
bella figlia mia
come forte ste core
batt

Io

sono la poesia
l'anello
di matrimonio

io
sono la terra
il peccato
la memoria
la ragione
del loro viaggio

io
ancora il respiro
le passioni
sprecate
l'interprete
la lingua straniera
la lingua madre

io
sempre
quella che organizza
il posto
il funerale
le parole
sulla pietra

from:

To The Men Who Write Goodbye Letters

In That Back Room

The man is killing time — there's nothing else.
—Robert Lowell

in that back room three flights up
with the rusted hot plate
burnt espresso pot
two unsteady chairs
you wrote the letter
all the bottles you had emptied
a glass courtyard for roaches
fat mice drunk on your leftovers
kept you company

there among the ghosts you inherited
the ones you invited to share your bed
all the poetry that kept you
sane or   not
you picked up the pen

there where the days were nights
the nights were days
you bled each drop   a leaky faucet
and she watched it stain everything

*

did you find time to fill the notebooks
with brilliant words
scribble the beginnings of song lyrics
document the great poems   beneath
the quarantined stars of that island
you escaped to   became

the god of your heart
breathtaking in your charm and solid flesh
there   you were anointed   conceded

but the Greek sky sometimes succumbs
to violent rain and even
the luckiest   most resilient
can lose their amulet in the rush for cover

*

she came across an old white cotton shirt
your face jumped inside her head
now she finds it necessary   to remember
whose shirt it is

it might have been yours
but you never made love in white cotton shirts
those were reserved for the lovers
you tortured her with

she's lonely   sad   losing her hair
needs to empty the drawers of everything
moving to a smaller space
not a physical one
one that will not keep her awake at night

perhaps it resembles the space you moved
into not long before you wrote that letter
when you had made up your mind

she's not sure
will walk around it a while
fold the white shirt   leave it on the chair

the last box you inhabited
the one behind the unclaimed books
that were never read   unpacked

she tried to unravel the two gold chains
your mother had given as gifts
wrapped in the lace handkerchief
one missing the medal

what to do with them   perhaps
Rachel will want them

but the photographs
will make a glowing fire

she recalls the story you told her
how images on paper
would haunt forever unless devoured in flames

how your mother burned funeral announcements
in the backyard fire pit

after finding your note she set on fire
all those cards of Christs   saints
and Virgin Marys

their charcoaled spirit carried away
with the wind

it didn't help her

you inherited all of the fears
your communion with ancestors
she was just there   to clean up
the mess

Lower East Side

he was a party boy
they all were then
before the city got clean
and the grunge got sold

he didn't hide it
he was proud
having a ball
showed us how it was done

the highs the lows
knockout blows
the women   drugs
screwed up loves

you can't be a
great party-boy with a conscience

it took him down

*

you should have hitched a ride
on that magic red balloon
with the little French boy
fleeing above the Paris sky

you might have both landed
on a stable cloud
with that lost dog   who needed you

the one Disney couldn't
fuck up

Reading Ferlinghetti in North Beach

any one of us cursed with memory
weeps for all that is passed

maybe it was a better time
a better place
maybe it   wasn't

but it is gone
taking with it our
quick legs   glorious skin

we cry into dry spaces
left behind

all over America
all that remains
the colours we brought

red — white — green

the rest is interpreted
re-interpreted
until the taste is dull

it will happen here
soon enough   this far north

we will be the America
they mistook us for

we will be so smoothed
of our moles and warts
will have spit out the last olive pit

we will be unrecognizable
we will belong to nothing

The Jump

the streetcars ran east and west on Danforth Avenue
before the subway was built

the Bloor line Leonardo laboured on
with other immigrant men
digging and laying tracks   took years

before it was done
we would ride the 'Rocket' all the way
to the viaduct on Sunday afternoons
get off at Broadview
walk the long bridge to look
into the deep green valley   below

Leonardo would raise his arms to the sky
and yell out his favourite word
libertà

*

the places we construct
bait us trap us into believing it is where
we might find   redemption

what deliverance does one find
laying flowers by a concrete slab
lighting wax candles to clay statues

in the end we jump
become air   fade

but this too may be a lie we offer ourselves

as we abandon favourite words
drop them over bridges   wait
to see how long it takes them to land

*

every immigrant story begins
with the elusive American dream
even if the dream is set in a Canadian landscape

if a dream can begin in five small rooms
of a semi-detached insulated-brick house
across from a Catholic church
in a city called   Toronto
on a street a man could never learn
to   pronounce
that's where it began for Leonardo

it ended on a Spring day   without clouds
when he flew over a bridge
the space below   wide
open   and   free

*

to be invisible   anonymous
is not a sin
merely a condition they allow
you can give your full name
pronounce it   spell it   print it clearly

but there is no guarantee they will   remember it

remembering is a dangerous exercise
a writer once wrote

Prodigies

i am surrounded by poets
who write for other poets

clever words fished from their
colossal complexities
their genius pool

the need to de-construct
and re-construct each other
a game without rules

ingenious assembly of vibrations
disguised as thoughts
borrowed from the left overs
of a favourite theorist

emotion is the enemy
well fondled

selective audiences enter
the exclusive lair
devour the wily developed skill
cunningly crafted
then exit when the bottles
are empty

Posers

they are eloquent
intellectuals   want-to-be poets

in the small circle of their assorted lives
stale as the clothes they hide in
watered down as the cheap liquor
they ingest for comfort

big words researched
to decrypt their theories

Friday night philosophers
Kafka Hegel   Wittgenstein
at the far table   Sartre cleans his specs
contemplates   the vacancies
we are   the rhetoric
of the absurd

dissecting ideologies and
the meaning of   art

somewhere beyond the full moon
Sylvia and Anne write poetry
nobody reads

Simone stepped out for a quick drag
smoke   rises   vanishes

To the Men Who Write Goodbye Letters

for Rosario

only fucked up romantics
write letters that become poems

you were young
your heart was too large
to accept anything less than   grace
anything less than   light
you crumbled

i am old now
you would not know me

i don't write letters
i organize   sanitize
i live in a clean house

my heart is overweight
with secrets and silence

i wish you had written
that letter to me back then
i might have convinced you that
        exiting
was the wrong thing to do

i might have talked you
into hanging around
so you too could have watched
the end of grace   the end of light

but you wanted to leave
when you were still   beautiful
didn't you

Charming the Demons

Should be learning how to die
　　rehearsing my final nakedness
　　　　—Luciano Iacobelli

he summons death
in all the spaces he occupies

catering to demons and angels
who hang about　　drifting
among the leaves and stones
of their final home

leaving his manufactured words
on bits of paper　　sticky notes
pasted onto famous　　graves

wanting to conjure the spirit
of great poets　　the legends

hoping the dust of their souls
will make him　　immortal

Mean Poems for my Father

my father never heard me read a poem
never heard my voice recite love
or anger
he heard the clicking of
typewriter keys late at night

the walls of our modest house were thin
and i typed all night long
on that Olivetti-Underwood he bought
for me at *Mastrangelo's* Gifts
when i was sixteen

the greatest gift he ever gave me
and i used it to write all those
mean poems about him

sometimes i typed out
my fears impossible dreams
collected them on paper
placed them in the bottom
drawer of my desk
the drawer with the miniature
silver key
the one i lost among the clutter

Dismantling the Dollhouse

for Giuliana

i would have played in the dollhouse
lived there   for you

become the princess in the ceramic cups
the one with the chocolate curls and pink lips

if i could have

i would have worn the Sicilian lace
rubbed myself raw with sweet lemons
become old with history
become   your history

if i could have

i would have pleased you
re-constructed dreams
of your ancient playgrounds
where daughters wore dresses
sons   did   not

instead the world will know
my heartaches   triumphs
offered in words on pages
to read   analyze

but some hurts i need
to keep for myself

The Medieval Tower

i was seven
the year i attempted to murder
Sister *Fiorenza*

cracked open a chunk of her forehead
with the steel pencil case
i lunged   as she sat at her desk
in her indifferent   sacred
superior space

toxic blood streamed
down her starched white bib
where the large crucifix had rested

Jesus bounced off her chest
like a slingshot
scraped her fleshy pale cheek
landed   undisturbed
on her bounded breasts

for seconds all i saw
was red white and black

my small heart   a volcano
erupting

i leaped over my desk
sprinted the few meters to the closet
where my sister   prisoner of some
venial sin
coughed   without breath
raising dust among the brooms
rags and rubbish of her cage

i grabbed her hand   pulled her out
two little scared rabbits
in ratty grey dresses
                                        running

there was no escape
only a circular *terrazzo*
a solid wall   a balcony
overlooking the wet mossy green
of the River *Liri*
Maria   trembling
in a puddle of pee and tears
don't be scared   i said
just roll like a ball

we jumped

They Tell Me

it is time to be old
—Ralph Waldo Emerson

the time has come
without invitation

to be pushing grandchildren
on park swings
putting high heel shoes in boxes
for Goodwill

clearing out closets
lighting a match to a
thousand photographs

leaving things clean
orderly
so sons and daughters will not
have to deal with the clutter

unrealized dreams
unnecessary in the end
they tell me

there are no grandchildren
the child says
mother get a dog

dogs frighten me

i will pack up the shoes
coats   dusty toys
empty the drawers of   things

but the photographs are proof
it all happened
the way i remember it

they will have to burn
later

Fading

my mother is shrinking
fading
becoming   air

delicate as the sparrows
she softens bread for
leaves on the chipped plate
in the garden
among her geraniums

neighbourhood cats   visit
stay longer than usual on her veranda
circle around her thin legs
afraid
she will not be there
for the next feeding

On Cumberland

strolling down Cumberland Avenue
in Yorkville
an October afternoon
i spotted a scarf in the window
of a fancy boutique

crimson red with white polka dots
just like the one mamma bought
for fifty cents
at Honest Ed's   years ago

nostalgia   or simply because
i love polka dots
i sauntered into the shop
draped it over my shoulders
looked in the designer mirror

it suited me
the way it had suited
my mother when
she wore it only   on Sundays

glanced at the price tag
mamma wouldn't approve

put it back on the shoulders
of the velvet mannequin
who wore it elegantly   without
memory

We Remain

papa dropped me off
every Saturday afternoon
our storefront playhouses
the Kenwood, the Doric
the Paradise

a dollar for the dream
a quarter for the popcorn
ordinary lives distracted
from the routine of
infinite toil and hustle
beneath the muted lights
the magic of romance   escape

neighbourhoods resist   centuries
patching cracks
conceiving new forms to celebrate
we are   the theater of our imagination
we remain

Dentr a 'sta cucina

(ciociaro dialect)

mamma m'aspetta
dentr a 'sta cucina
ogni giorn
neue e gele
sole e acqua
calle o fridd
m'aspetta

la cazzarola è pronta
bolle
i piatt e bicchier
sopra a i mantil che le rose
tutt pronto e apparecchiat
le pane c'a fatt stamattina
miezz a i tauline

Inside This Kitchen

(translation)

mamma waits
inside this kitchen
every day
snow or ice
sun or rain
hot or cold
            she waits

the pot is ready
boiling
dishes and glasses set
on the tablecloth with the red roses
everything is ready and waiting
the bread she baked
this morning
in the center of the table

Not So Catholic

my sister is off again travelling the globe
pilgrimages
                    shrines

sacred beads   blessings around the world
making sure the soul will be well   protected
for eternity

holy mothers and saints   appear
in faraway places
welcome her devotion   her faith
the rhetoric of words and wallets

i sit with our mother each day
on a well-worn chair
in her kitchen   with one window
looking on to the garden
her hand-washed laundry   drying

between coffee and orange slices
i listen to her   history
our history

my soul   less secure
in its destination

First Love

my mother's first love
had Sicilian eyes

took her to his island
across the strait of Messina

a place where the volcano
still smokes   rumbles

in the hills of *Chiaramonte*
high above the sea
she would find home

the shoeless *ciociara* girl
who had filled his eyes
that Sunday in the piazza
back in 1943

he made a promise to return
when the guns were quiet

that September when
the sky was still
the world breathed again
he walked the gravel road
brought her ripe figs
white lace

the Mediterranean blue
in his Sicilian eyes

Good Daughters

It was a year of great sadness
in the garden
—Jenny Bornholdt

good daughters are caretakers
keepers of secrets

know the best hiding places
share only the   necessary

monsoons will come
seasons of hail and harvest
inevitable
good daughters   organize
learn   to lie well

This Is My Pain

> Even you, if you knew
> How this darkness soaks me through and through
> —D.H. Lawrence

my mother's arms have become skin
only skin
arms that held my sister and me
our children
no longer
lift a newborn easily

my mother's hands
slender   silent
on the bedsheet

her gold wedding band loose
beneath the knuckle and curved bone
i twirl it around and around
like a toy
her faint heartbeat
in my palm

tomorrow i will paint her nails
a dusky rose
her favourite shade

*

i watch her enter another space
in and out of sleep
her breath   struggling

alone with her
with fear and prayer
all i have   is tears

my fingers
twirling a thin circle of gold

Ten Days in January

this month defines darkness
even in its white disguise

from the sixth floor hospital window
my mother stares   at falling flakes
as they melt into
the sidewalk of Church Street

the thin ice breath   of January
seeps in beneath the glass pane

wrapped in my wool scarf
i sit on the rigid chair   for hours
lean on the window sill

watch my mother
watch snowflakes disappear

*

she seems smaller today
in daylight   her large eyes
behind the trusted sunglasses
she has trained to give her comfort

her lids open and close constantly
but she won't give in to fatigue
won't give in to   sleep

her body turned against her
one rogue cell gone   wild
is all it takes   the doctor said

but her mind is clear
her heart resilient

*

she is thinking of Spring
the garden in May
will she be there to turn the soil
prepare the seedlings   reprimand me
when i use   the wrong tool
dig the wrong sized hole

the snowflakes are thicker today
she removes her sunglasses
wipes them clean
tells me to water the plants
keep the flowers alive

i am not the gardener
but i will keep the geraniums
in the clay pots by the window

my husband will have to be
custodian   of the garden
he understands seeds and soil
the way mamma does

Language

when my mother died
so did our language

the one we spoke
each day at the kitchen table
each night by the hum
of the television
on the telephone   between visits

the language that dropped
from the open window above
her garden
while she pruned and tied and watered

an old language
perfect for prayers she whispered
songs she sang

it lived between us
like the child we both love

now i must slide my fingers over this
miracle of technology
to hear her   voice

this new world has no need for
old languages
but while i am here
i will hold it safe
in the limbo of my gut

Lingua

(translation)

quando è morta mamma
è morta anche la nostra lingua

quella che parlavamo ogni giorno
insieme
ogni giorno al tavolo in cucina
ogni sera sotto il rumore della televisione
al telefono

quella lingua che scappava
dalla finestra e arrivava in giardino
mentre piantava, allacciava, annaffiava

una vecchia lingua
perfetta per le preghiere che recitava
le canzoni che cantava

una lingua che viveva fra noi
come quella bimba che amiamo
ora devo scivolare le dita
su questo miracolo di tecnologia
per sentire la sua   voce

questo nuovo mondo non ha bisogno
di vecchie lingue
ma mentre sono qui
la tengo sicura nel limbo
del mio ventre

The Last Room

when we sat in your kitchen
with espresso   or wine
endless dishes filled
with whatever had taken
your fancy   that day
we never would have imagined
the last room of your life
would be   the sixth floor
of a building on Church Street
south of Bloor
in this city that has pretended
to be   home
for fifty nine years

the last room of your life
has large windows without a view
only   January flakes

wish i could have given you hills
plump with   rain
the blue of the Ionian sea
tall umbrella pines
brought you   ripe purple figs
and sweet lemons of a
                    Sicilian summer

Dressing Gown

in my mother's bathroom
behind the door
her rose velvet dressing gown
with satin pockets
hangs on a copper hook
waiting for her nightly rituals

the spaces around the sink
occupied with her
creams   her perfumes
little packets of lavender
in the crystal dish
blue comb and brush

those dreaded pills
for cholesterol   she hated
too large to swallow

if i leave them untouched
she may be back for them

The Garden Mother Left Me

last year i turned the soil for you
pushed that spade down
into dry ground
lifted the chunks   .beat that clay
raked
watered till it was smooth

you watched
sitting beneath the green umbrella
hating   every second
you could not do it yourself

impatient
couldn't resist the   challenge
lifted yourself from the plastic chair
in your pain and blue wool slippers
took possession   of the spade
moved me out of the way
showed me   the proper technique
i could never get right

it's that weekend in May again
the umbrella in place
your empty chair beneath its shade
the wool slippers folded

this year it's all up to me

Identity

my mother did not fall
into sentiment   or romance
                              easily
had no doubts
knew   who she was

took care of the necessary
without complaints
believed in the   good

my mother loved without needing
                                         returns
set aside her dreams
replaced them   with prayer
duty

unlike me   i question everything
find few answers
i cry in the daylight
        my mother cried in the dark

Surrender

Le tombe le case … cuore cuore non ti fermare.	The graves the houses … heart heart don't stop beating.

—Rocco Scotellaro

today is my birthday
one we label significant
as if others weren't

this one will allow me discounts
on drugs and toiletries
movie tickets and bus rides

it has provoked a need
to reassemble a mosaic
before all the pieces
are disbursed lost

before history will have been
re-assembled
labeled miscellaneous

i no longer shift or plan
for the changing climate
the contents of drawers closets
remain in place unruffled
regardless of weather

winter
has calmed to a simple irritation
time ignores the seasons

i return to the old neighbourhood
far from where my home is now
to re-discover a street   paved
by my ancestors   where i once played

wide and endless   it seemed then
when my name was different
i walked it much faster

Die So I Can Write About It

i don't recall who wrote the line
some poet an important one
perhaps

i forget a lot of things lately
makes it is easier now
to forgive

you left for a good reason
i think i hope
maybe you needed a first kill
to write

was i too loud
fat awkward
my voice too clear it frightened you

you needed to be the clever one
creative ingenious
living your happiness
as a myth a parable

was i too foreign you wanted a
piece of me to complete your heart
but i hadn't been murdered yet

you danced me to the stairwell
i lacked grace stumbled
was it your hand that pushed me
then held me down sunlight
on a tired body
a vacancy light enough
to dispose

we wander backwards
towards our sins   surveying
find only the grief   guilt
in all the hollow spaces

Sometimes It Gets Very Dark

for Susan (1950-2020)

she lived in a house with a yellow bird
a faithful old dog named Bailey
and all the accumulated dreams of a
happy life

if anyone knew the probable
origins   of   happiness
she might have come the closest
i was too practical
too catholic then
saw the sadness in everything

her sky was always blue
any rain   any storm
any lost dog or broken soul
was welcome

'beautiful'
was a favourite word
until it all got very dark and
beautiful things   shattered
fragments too difficult to mend

she walked away on a winter night
starless
into the forest she loved
and by the banks of a river
chose a different way   home

January Twenty-One

è *dentro la tua grazia che nasce la mia angoscia*
(it is inside your grace that my anguish is born)
—Pier Paolo Pasolini

the eleventh of January   my birthday
i took you to emergency

ten days   i sat beside you
did not move
my knees stiff   turning to stone

watched you tiptoe away
from me   we talked
held hands   prayed
waited

i'm tired ma   i'm really tired
while you sleep i will go lie down
just a few hours   i'll be back soon

ten days you   waited
this Sunday morning while
the bells of St. Francis
announced the eight o'clock mass
i drove the sleepy streets
of Toronto   returning to you
but you too   were tired
you could not wait for me

Locking the Door

Tread lightly, she is near
Under the snow,
Speak gently, she can hear
The daisies grow.
—Oscar Wilde

Eliot misunderstood April
January
is the cruelest month

mamma chose the coldest
to lie beside papa's bones
forever

trees stripped for winter
leaving birds homeless

only plastic wreaths propped
on stone markers bouquets
that never die in full bloom

i am left to empty my mother's
house of all the years
language history

take down all the Christs
she'd hung with devotion
leave the walls clean for
other pieties
lock the door one last time

New poems/2020

Women cry more easily because
they still carry so much
of the sea in their bodies.
—Mary di Michele, *Immune to Gravity*

Quarantined

from my window
above the still garden
                                        i stare
at the boundaries of my world

April enters the back gate
without a reception
an intruder creeping quietly
to claim a space

i cannot help but think about   God
His absence   or
                                                    His presence
both concepts   equally
frightening   to embrace
His handiwork   obstructed
barricaded
                              delayed
the balance of order and beauty
in disorder

concealed in my sanitized purgatory
through the glass pane i search for
                                                       my god

there among the weightless clouds
of a new Spring   he must be
carefree   and   hiding

Rome/2020/The Lost Year

no one is sitting beneath the
umbrella pines
no new coins dropped in the
fountain of dreams and returns

a scattering of neglected souls
drift aimlessly in the holy square
waiting for the miracle
that blessing from the
                    sacred window

solitary guards and saints
                    at attention
no Caesars   no Gods
only ghosts   are free
to roam the Coliseum

Re-visiting the Street of Widows

the street of widows is almost
                                        vacant
wives are following husbands
reluctantly   as always

mamma was one of the last
she did not want to leave
but time has no   compassion
neither has   death

grandchildren have abandoned
basement kitchens   moved on
to designer spaces   airy lofts
replaced the cravings for chicken soup
and meatballs

while fashionable restaurants
cash in on the   nostalgia
of '*nonna* recipes'
homes are cleansed sanitized
                                  of the old
they are simply real estate
made ready and   modern
for new and different baptisms

Kapiti Island

you bring it all with you
in your knees   your shoulders
it's there inside your head
beneath the balding spot
in the aches you cannot define
the ones you cannot assign to
reasons

'i will forget when i get there'
but you never do

you look at a tree   you are climbing it
                                    you are ten
you see a church   the guilt returns

the gnarled hands of an old woman
shape everything   while
rising dough fattens   slowly
before baking

shadows of mortality
track your steps   no exits
the uneasy heart searching for
sanctuary
                        eclipsing in the distance

you try to describe the sea
as the writer Toibin
did in his book
that one story you loved
but you are not   of the sea

the hills that claim you were
always too tall to climb
too far away to describe

now   you are here
learning to love an   ocean
an island   in the pacific
under the long white cloud

City Bench

for Vincenzo

once upon a time we were the fairy tale
assorted lives
sculpting supermen dreams
with mortar and brick
glass and concrete
with paper and pen and
                                        cameras

whittling bark into inspired shapes
mixing colours beyond their
natural   brilliance

on rest days we strolled
the sidewalks we designed
the roads we constructed
making love
                    babies
                                    and plans

this neighbourhood will not disturb
the world
we are   short-term
a memory   fading
sit here a while on this bench
i have built many like these
                                    in my lifetime
have an ice-cream before it melts

In the Thrift Shop

my mother's dishes
are on the second shelf
$2.99 for each plate
the ones with the little flowers
and the gold rim

i packed her   kitchen
in cardboard boxes
wrapped each plate   each glass
each crystal bowl in newspaper

all the espresso cups
little spoons folded between
the linen tablecloths that
had crossed the ocean in a trunk
gave them all away to the
thrift shop

somewhere in a stranger's home
in this Canadian city
my mother's kitchen still lives

Modern Wedding in a City Loft

no one really noticed
grandmother   was there
had her hair done for the occasion
wore a blue dress and matching purse
brand new shoes with a little heel
gold earrings from her own wedding day
no one saw them   no one looked
commented on their vintage design
no one spoke her   language

they sat her at the   special table
well behaved and quiet
she observed the festivities
the intricate tattoos on the bride
the purple hair and jeweled nose ring
the officiate wore suspenders

no prayers or hymns
the God she knew   wasn't invited
she came just the same   so proud

brought her eighty five years
the envelope with cash money
smiled   waited patiently
until someone drove her
home

These Sad Days

these sad days
will not remember
how a touch   soothes
how a kiss returns the heart
to that first time
life shop lifted   concealed
postponed
yet the sun lights the sky
the robin builds a nest
daffodils   sprout

among the untidiness of our
mistakes
truths are scattered waiting
to be uncovered   shaken
aroused   something new

All We Are Is a Short Story

to be cursed with mediocrity
a sin   without baptism
or redemption

she sees a woman without   escape
life without   the truth   of anything
merely   commonplace

a badly structured sentence   loitering
in a paragraph of a second-rate novel
dust laden   unopened
tossed in the dollar bin of the Goodwill
among the   reductions
of what the world does not need
                                        or want

nameless identities   collected
in words   forgotten faces
Arbus   photographs

this irrelevant sequence of
waking   breathing
this routine of water and soap
                              coffee and milk
clocks and calendars
the absurdity of all that is   and isn't
still   the lie she sometimes
                                        indulges

unexpected moments of yearning
a sun drunk red tomato
the sugary awakening of a ripe peach

a swelling in the skin   to be touched
to savour   the invasion

if she had one wicked wish
to be completely
                                        beautiful
and stupid
it might guarantee   happiness
and the forgiveness of   sin

A Long Long Time

the woods spread out before me
in their tall greens and yellows
every cloud swollen to its softest
every clear lake conquered in blue

this country where i landed
fills my heart to the brim
its largeness will not end
i have lived here a long
                                        long time

while my soul still hungers for ripe
                                              sweet figs
for the cool shade of an umbrella pine
it cannot refuse the unsparing beauty
the generosity of this home

The Umbrella Pines

along the dirt road by the River *Liri*
the pines guide me back

when my legs were young
i was the quick lizard
climbed without the need of breath
in search of the boy
who lived among the branches

but there is no young defiant
Baron in the trees

who welcomes me   now

only the broad green perfumed heads
on the giant furrowed trunks
majestic   regal still
their dizzying fragrance
a downpour on my veiled skin

i return with a heavy casket
of vagrant memories
without a plot where they might rest

Christmas/Natale

my mother's hands   at Christmas
were always busy   mixing
sweet dough with raisins vanilla
                                        and rum
sprinkling icing sugar on lemon cookies
grinding almonds and walnuts
into a cauldron of pure honey

changing the water on the salted cod
for days
while Jesus kept watch
                              above the fridge

the egg noodles she kneaded
worked with her palms till the dough
was smooth yellow   and silken
long beautiful ribbons laid naked
and gold on the linen tablecloth

and she did all with a song
'*tu scendi dalle stelle*'
there are new cooks
in my mother's house   this year
i handed over the keys   to strangers
who will never know the love   left
well baked   inside her stove

my hands are busy in my own kitchen
                                        this Christmas
i am the cook
without Jesus above my fridge
without mamma's song

i hope the noodles turn out light
and the cod is not too   salty

County Fireflies

maybe i brought them with me
all those years ago
tucked into the wine glasses
mamma packed in that heavy trunk
or they hid in the suitcase
between the clean underwear
among the linens *nonna* had folded
the ones she had initialed in red thread

perhaps they snuck inside all those
little boxes of   nothing
we couldn't leave behind
landed here on this tender night
June   in Prince Edward County
the hush of a rented country house
a drowsy fragrant garden
                        i watch them flicker about

between memory   and nostalgia
there are tiny flying stars in my eyes
i know there is   no Italy
there is no Canada
only miniature transient lights
seducing   possessing the world's
night skies

Good-night Federico

happy 100th birthday

you believe art has something to say
it needs no explanation it must simply
'move you'
but you love to lie don't you Federico
to amuse to imagine
to dream
dreams are your truth your magic

but what is art what is life
if not a dream we express in the light

the child inside never fears
there are no mistakes in fantasy
you play with memory and ideology
crafting style with madness and clowns

the perfect moment may never come
so we must be ready to create it
to exist in the minutes of fancy
and lies

you have said that 'passion is life'
life is real and unreal
no borders to define what is lived
or imagined so we enter
your cities

your women your men
they are the *affreschi* of celluloid and sound

they breathe your divinity without the need
of a god

but you are cruel at times aren't you Federico
maestro of tease and contradiction
                    a lover and a traitor
on every ship every train in every fountain
we bathe with each romance
                         of fools

"there is no beginning —— there is no end"
allora,   *buona notte Federico …*
                         a domani.

# Acknowledgements

I want to acknowledge the support of the Canada Council, Ontario Arts Council and Guernica Editions for their support and dedication to the arts. For their continued championing of new and diverse voices

Thank you to Anthony Julian Tamburri of the John Calandra Institute, New York who was the first to review my book *Italian Women and Other Tragedies* in 1995 and who generously took time to write the preface to *This Way Home.*

To poet Rob Rolfe, to Paolo Frasca, University of Toronto, Teresa Russo, University of Brock and UofT, Karleen Pendleton Jimenez, Trent University and Anna Mongibello, Università di Napoli Orientale thank you for your continued encouragement, your friendship and the time you dedicated reading and endorsing this collection. I am honoured by your words.

A thank you to Guernica's founder Antonio D'Alfonso for publishing my first books of poetry, and to Michael Mirolla and Connie Guzzo-McParland for continuing to take Guernica Editions forward into new territories. Also a sincere thank you to Quattro Books and Lyrical Myrical Press for my earlier publications. And to Luciana Ricciutelli and the team at Inanna publications for my book of short fiction. I am forever grateful.

To the many students who have welcomed me into their classrooms and to their tireless teachers who have allowed me to share in their visions and their thoughts on my work, on life and literature and much more, I have treasured every moment. I wish you success in life and in the choices you make.

To all my friends, you know who you are, I cherish you.

To my sister, my nieces and nephew, and my wonderful large extended family (in Canada, Italy and New Zealand), who make all things possible, necessary and fun, I love you.

To my daughter Gia and to William, my husband Andrew, nothing would make sense without all of you in my life.

And a thank you to the late poet Pier Giorgio Di Cicco whom I met in 1977 when we were young and all the words were jumbled and confused in my head and my heart. His poems helped me to decipher my own and to find their place in the world.

Lastly I want to acknowledge and thank my editor and publisher at Inanna Publications, my friend, Luciana Ricciutelli for all her support. Luciana died while I was working on this collection for Guernica. A unique, beautiful and intelligent woman and professional who believed in my work and in the work of the women's voices she published with a commitment and energy that was endless. Her beloved press, Inanna, freed many into a literary world that would not otherwise have known we existed. You leave a void that will never be filled.

About the Author

Gianna Patriarca was born in Ceprano, Frosinone, Italy. She came to Canada as a child in 1960. She is a graduate of York University with a degree in English Literature, B. of Education and a minor in Italian. She is an award-winning author of 11 books, poetry, fiction and children's literature. She also writes a variety of articles for magazine publications. Her work is extensively anthologized, produced for Canada Stage, TV Ontario, CHIN, Telelatino and for CBC radio drama. Her work is featured in numerous documentaries including *Pier 21, The Italian Canadians, Three Women Adopting Lines Adapting Lives, Enigmatico*. Her work is internationally recognized and appears on the course list of universities in USA, Canada and Italy. She was the first recipient of the Arts and Cultural award from the Italian Chamber of Commerce in Ontario in 2010. Her first book, *Italian Women and Other Tragedies* 1994, is in its fourth printing. Gianna lives in Toronto where she has taught elementary school. She is working on a novel.

Books by Gianna Patriarca

Italian Women and Other Tragedies
Daughters for Sale
Ciao Baby
The Invisible Woman
What My Arms Can Carry
Nonna and the Girls Next Door
My Etruscan Face
Donne Italiane ed Altre Tragedie
Too Much Love
All My Fallen Angelas
To The Men Who Write Goodbye Letters

This book is made of paper from well-managed FSC® - certified forests, recycled materials, and other controlled sources.

MIX
Paper from responsible sources
FSC® C103567
FSC
www.fsc.org

PCF

BIO GAS ENERGY

PERMANENT